The Book as Art

Foreword

The Book as Art welcomes readers to the amazing world of artists' books. Treasures of intricate craftsmanship, artists' books take every possible form, include every artistic medium and method of bookmaking, and engage every subject from food and family to politics and poetry, familiar tales to wild fantasy. A majority of gifted book artists are women, owing perhaps to women's attraction to storytelling, intimacy, and collaboration.

One of the finest collections of artists' books in the world resides at the National Museum of Women in the Arts in Washington, D.C. The collection contains over eight hundred unique and limited-edition volumes by such renowned artists as Mirella Bentivoglio, Meret Oppenheim, May Stevens, and Claire Van Vliet.

This outstanding collection was carefully assembled over twenty years by Krystyna Wasserman, director of the museum's Library and Research Center from 1982 to 2002 and currently its curator of book arts. She has been a pioneer in the collection and study of this art form, which has gained in stature and international interest during the past two decades. Since 1987, Ms. Wasserman has curated annual exhibitions of artists' books that have attracted a dedicated audience of aficionados and introduced many new admirers to the medium.

On the occasion of the museum's twentieth anniversary, we are proud to present this book and a major exhibition of 108 fine artists' books from this remarkable collection.

Judy L. Larson
Director, National Museum of Women in the Arts

Acknowledgments

The Book as Art: Artists' Books from the National Museum of Women in the Arts is published on the occasion of the museum's twentieth anniversary. I find this deeply gratifying, as I do the fact that the accompanying exhibition is presented as the major exhibition of the fall 2006 season. This lavish edition and an entire floor of the museum dedicated to the display of artists' books affirms my belief that this art form deserves recognition and exposure equal to that of other media. For sharing this belief I thank Wilhelmina Cole Holladay, NMWA's founder and chair of the board. I am also deeply grateful to Judy L. Larson, the museum's director, and Susan Fisher Sterling, deputy director and chief curator.

My gratitude also goes to all who provided financial support for this publication, the exhibition, and the acquisition of artists' books for the permanent collection. Thank you for your active interest, generosity, and artistic and intellectual affinity. Among these contributors are: Diane K. Blumberg, Roma Dillon-Smyth Crocker, Betty G. Edelson, Lorraine Grace, Wilhelmina Cole Holladay, Marianne J. Huber, Lynn M. Johnston, Margaret Johnston, Sharon Keim, Fred H. Levin and Nancy Livingston, Barbara Mitchell, The Honorable Mary V. Mochary, Nelleke Nix, Nancy O'Malley, Mary Perrin, and June Rosner. A special note of thanks is due to the Texas State Committee of NMWA for acquiring for the museum the spectacular artists' book *Beauty.Chaos*.

The fundraising efforts for this book and exhibition were spearheaded by Judy L. Larson and the NMWA development department, and assisted by Carol Lascaris, president of the NMWA Endowment. I am deeply grateful to Angela Gilchrist, former director of the development department, whose interest in the publication of this book resulted in a major contribution from a gracious and generous donor. I also wish to thank Erin Harms, associate director of corporate, foundation, and government support, for her fundraising efforts.

The creative spirit behind this book has been Elizabeth Nicholson, managing editor at NMWA. Working with a talented and imaginative editor is a distinct privilege, and I am grateful for this most enjoyable experience. While doing my share of the writing for this book, with many days of struggle with the complexities of a language I was not born into, I was sustained by Elizabeth's warmth and friendship. The wonderful NMWA editorial team included Vivian Djen, a brilliant young woman who helped organize the text, images, and rights for more than a hundred artists' books; NMWA editor Kerry Folan, who assisted with manuscript editing and proofing; and Nancy Eickel, who assisted with copyediting.

NMWA is especially grateful for the enthusiasm, patience, and faith of Kevin Lippert, Nancy Eklund Later, Clare Jacobson, Jan Haux, and the staff of Princeton Architectural Press. Their efforts toward the publication of this book are too many to count, but each is highly valued and deeply appreciated.

For their creativity and hard work on the installation of the exhibition, I would like to thank registrar Catherine Bade, chief preparator Greg Angelone, and preparator Quint Marshall. And to the rest of the NMWA staff, too numerous to name here, who assisted with the realization of this book, the exhibition, educational programs, publicity, and special events, my deepest and most sincere thanks.

I am extremely grateful to two talented writers who have lent their intellectual gifts to this volume. Johanna Drucker—a book artist, scholar of artists' books, and professor of English and director of media studies at the University of Virginia—arrived one Sunday from Charlottesville to review the works selected for the exhibition. The insightful essay she subsequently wrote provides an analysis of the medium from the feminist perspective and positions artists' books in historical context. Book artist, educator, and best-selling novelist Audrey Niffenegger wrote an introduction to this book that is of a more personal nature. She extols the importance of books and art in her life and, from her unique perspective, answers the question: What does it mean to make a book?

My special affinity is for all of the artists whose works are included in this book, because their contributions form the core of the project and are thus the most important. In addition to creating astounding and beautiful books, the artists have also written candid texts that provide valuable insight into their work. I also wish to acknowledge the hundreds of artists whose works reside in the NMWA collection. I regret that I could not include every one of their remarkable books in this volume and in the exhibition.

The excellence, artistic flair, and endless patience of Lee Stalsworth, photographer for most of the images in this book, is very gratefully acknowledged. I also send a special note of thanks to Nancy Lutz for editing the first draft of my essay. I am grateful to Carla Tonini for her help with Italian translations and for transporting from Bologna Donatella Franchi's artist's book for the exhibition. Many thanks to Miriam Laughlin and to Robert M. Laughlin, curator of Mesoamerican and Caribbean ethnology at the Smithsonian Institution, for introducing me to two books of poetry by Mayan women designed by Ámbar Past and published by Taller Leñateros, a book art center in San Cristóbal de las Casas, Mexico.

Finally, I wish to thank my husband Paul Wasserman for all his support and love.

Krystyna Wasserman
Curator of Book Arts, National Museum of Women in the Arts

creative graphic work in book form. By the end of the decade, many women artists and writers had established their identities through their book projects. These included Frances Butler, Betsy Davids, Warja Lavater, Bea Nettles, and Claire Van Vliet.

An artist's book is a work of art that is conceived and executed as a book and does not exist in any other form or format. It might make use of images, texts, and any and all means of production—photography, painting, drawing, collage, metalwork, stitching, beading—both hand- and machine-driven. It is important to mention that, despite dire predictions that computer technology will be the end of the codex, digital means of production in fact provide a host of affordable print and processing capabilities for the makers of books.

Female practitioners have been highly influential in the growing field of artists' books, both by virtue of their art and through their careers as teachers and mentors. To find the reasons why women artists are drawn to the book form—a complex format that is difficult to exhibit and laborious to produce—one must consider the power of books to confer authority upon their makers. The cultural icon of a book remains a potent sign, even in this era of new technology. At the same time, the experience of making and reading books occurs in a private and meditative space, amounting to immersion in a virtual world. For the woman artist, the paradoxical private-public nature of books serves dual desires—for self-protection and recognition, for the preservation of modesty and the display of competence.

The activities associated with bookmaking are socially coded in a positive way as feminine. The sewing of pages, deft handling of glue and paste, detailed drawings, and carefully cut figures and openings reflect the supposedly feminine traits of attention to detail and a disposition toward aesthetic pleasure in the selection and combination of materials. Certainly women artists enjoy the tactile satisfaction of holding a book and the inexhaustible pleasures of making one. It is not by accident that we find so many materials in their works: doilies, pieces of silk, fragments of kimonos, clothing scraps, soap, photographs, small scrolls, jars and other containers, reused stamps, buttons, ribbon, and snippets of this and that. For the power of stuff, like that of stories and images, connects us to the lived through the signs of use and wear that measure the precious connection of memory to experience.

Women, acculturated to the language of personal voice, have frequently used diaries and journals as companions to their inner lives. Famous examples abound: Anne Frank, Anais Nin, Virginia Woolf, Marie Bashkirtseff, and Harriet Jacobs, to name a few. Not all bookworks are conceived as repositories of secrets, nor are most confidences so disposed meant to end in a book-shaped tomb. Books are inherently optimistic; they express the belief that communication will be received later and elsewhere, a time-released epistle to an eager reader somewhere, sometime. The habit of confessional writing is a bid for exposure and attention, even as it serves as a means of reflection and complaint, of self-involved and sometimes unintentional disclosure.

A highly personal thread runs through many of the works in this book, and throughout the broader collection from which it draws. Travels, dreams, loss, family life, relationships, and motherhood are major themes. So are activist issues in the tradition of feminist works from earlier eras. Themes such as abuse, violence, war, and genocide provide impetus for bookworks. The fate of the Earth and the inhumanity of culture are topics that motivate women to expression and action.

The overwhelming force of this medium is its power to give form to the stories according to which women imagine their lives will be led. The symbolic orders of imagery and text shape experience into knowledge and then memory. The accounts on these pages show the limits of the plausible. What kind of lives can women lead? Can they imagine? What are the stories that can be told about those lives? These tales and images are passed across lines of culture, generation, and history, through an ongoing process that synthesizes individual and collective expression.

Often the stories are quite ordinary, such as in Susan Allix's *The Beach* (pp. 140-41), where the images suggest an uneventful idyll and the text is made only of punctuation—all pauses and stops signifying a space apart from the rest of life. Sometimes the stories are presented in their own miniature theatrical environments, as in Carol Barton's *Five Luminous Towers* (pp. 132-33), illuminated with a small bulb, or Mary Bennett's *German Egypt* (p. 131), a transformation of a travel book into a solid geometric form. Brenda Watson's *Comment attirer les oiseaux?* (pp. 54-55), contains its vistas within the wingspan of its iconically shaped pages. The book comments on the view we have of the world we are privileged to inhabit.

Many women artists are committed to the reinterpretation of tradition. Sometimes these are traditions from which they were once excluded, which they reclaim through the act of re-creation. Béatrice Coron's reworking of a poem by François Villon and Jenny Hunter Groat's homage to Wendell Berry create a dialogue that might not have been possible in another era, but which renews a cultural legacy from a fresh perspective. *A Merz Sonata* (pp. 160-61), Debra Weier's tribute to Kurt Schwitters, is an expression of Weier's own claim to participation in experimental collage and poetics.

Many of the books reflect a personal experience, and some of the most moving are simple and recycle objects from everyday life. Allison Cooke Brown's *Teatimes* (p. 63), is a diary written on teabags placed in order in their box. Other books are playful, as in the case of Pat Oleszko's *Glove Story* (pp. 38-39), which takes its language from the flirtatious texts of personal ads. There are many painful tales, such as Yani Pecanins' *Los dos lados* (p. 107) and Lois Morrison's book about children titled *Endangered Species* (pp. 104-5). All in some sense participate in the suggestion posed by Ann Kresge's title, *Shadow Play* (p. 170-71): a book is a virtual space in which the symbols and structures of expression perform for us and through us, in our reading and engagement of the work.

No single, simple correlation exists between books and their thematic and expressive possibilities. Expanses of mind and heart, exterior gestures and internal journeys exist alongside works that are means of interacting or meant as intervention. Books are spaces in which to make community as well as places to be left alone. The unseen engines of any book's creation are complex, inevitably bound to the education and socialization of women, shaping women's expectations and relation to authority and power, their intimate and public concepts of themselves as artists, their access to means of production and expression. We may read back from the abundant evidence, the beauties and treasures laid before our eyes, into those networks of activity and motivation. We may also read forward into the tremendous impact and effect of these works as statements that stand on their own, realized and objectified embodiments of that intimate authority each artist claims as her own in the making of a book.

References:

Betty Bright, *No Longer Innocent: Book Art in America 1960-1980* (New York: Granary Books, 2005).

Rebecca W. Davidson, *Unseen Hands: Women Printers, Binders, and Book Designers*, Princeton University Library, Graphic Arts Collection, online exhibition, http://libweb2.princeton.edu/rbsc2/ga/unseenhands/ (November 2, 2005).

Laura Sue Fuderer, *Women Printers and Booksellers: A Checklist of Sources* http://www.sharpweb.org/bibwomen.htm (November 2, 2005).

Phyllis Maguire, "Unseen Hands: Women in the Print Shop," *U.S. 1 Newspaper*, March 12, 2003, http://www.princetoninfo.com/200303/30312p05.html (November 2, 2005).

Daniel Berkeley Updike, *Printing Types: Their History, Forms and Use* (Cambridge, Mass.: Belknap Press, 1962).

museum I enjoyed some great advantages, the foremost being a lasting friendship with its founder, whose staunch support for all library-related projects has remained unwavering through the years. In my capacity as director of the museum's Library and Research Center (LRC), I had nearly total freedom to develop the library in ways I believed best served its users—scholars and generalists who were eager to study the neglected contributions of women to art history. When the time came to move the library collection to its permanent home in the museum's newly renovated New York Avenue building, I immersed myself in the task of space planning. It was 1983 and I had just seen my first exhibition of artists' books at the Cleveland Institute of Art. Enchanted, I was determined to present equally exciting exhibitions in our future library. I lobbied successfully for a reading room large and versatile enough to accommodate artists' book exhibitions. The library's grand opening on September 21, 1987 included *The Book as Art I*, my first show of artists' books. The opening featured a lecture by prominent artist Claire Van Vliet of Janus Press, a star in the artists' book pantheon. It was an auspicious beginning.

The museum's collection of artists' books was small at first, but from the outset Mrs. Holladay embraced the idea of collecting and exhibiting artists' books. An early trip to New York to visit Tony Zwicker, one of the first dealers and enthusiasts of artists' books in the United States, resulted in the acquisition of Meret Oppenheim's *Caroline* (pp. 154–55). The bittersweet memory of this purchase has stayed with me to this day. A sublime book of poetry and etchings, *Caroline* was published in a limited edition of eighty-nine copies by Edition Fanal in Basel. It would be one of Oppenheim's last works. Though she showed no signs of illness, on the occasion of her seventy-second birthday on October 6, 1985 the artist announced to her friends, "I will die before the first snow." Five weeks later, on November 15, she died of a heart attack, after signing all copies of the book at her publisher's party.

Long before NMWA's official opening, artists here and abroad were eager to show their support for its singular mission, and book artists were no exception. In 1985 we received letters from Mirella Bentivoglio and Elisabetta Gut, artists from Rome who had read about the newly established museum in the Italian press. Each offered us the choice of one of her *libri-oggetti* (book-objects). We selected two books for the museum: *À Malherbe* by Bentivoglio and *Libro-seme* (p. 58) by Gut—the first of the library's international book art acquisitions.

As a young private museum we often lacked the means to foster the book art program. A creative solution to this problem was the establishment in 1989 of the Library Fellows program. The Library Fellows support the creation of artists' books by funding an annual grant awarded to the book artist who submits the best proposal for a new work. The annual contributions from the Library Fellows, along with the sales revenue from the award-winning books, have made possible regular exhibitions of artists' books at the museum and the acquisition of new artists' books for the collection. This dynamic funding program, coupled with the generosity of our donors, has allowed the National Museum of Women in the Arts to become one of the foremost repositories of artists' books in the world.

As director of the LRC for twenty years (1982–2002), I curated the annual exhibitions collectively known as *The Book as Art*. Over the years, these developed a considerable audience of artists' book aficionados. In 2003 I retired as director of the LRC and was appointed curator of book arts. Due to the successful growth of the collection and an outpouring of interest in the genre, exhibitions of artists' books have been given space in the museum's galleries and equal status to the other visual arts.

In the course of my work, my greatest joy has been interactions with the artists themselves. I have visited presses and studios all over the world, often designing my vacations around the places where book artists live and work. To my surprise, none of the artists I visited created books on her kitchen table—a popular myth from the early days of the feminist art movement. The notion was that women gravitated to the artists' book medium because, unlike their male counterparts, they could not afford large studio spaces. The fact is that artists make books everywhere—in their homes, studios, classrooms, and print shops—because they love making books. They make art for love's sake.

I have also noted with satisfaction that many book artists live well, often surrounded by beautiful landscapes, and more than a few cultivate gardens. It was M. L. Van Nice, a book artist from Somerville, Massachusetts, who explained to me the significance of a garden by comparing it to a library. Van Nice believes that cultivating the mind through reading is not unlike tending a garden, and that books are "just another form of fertilizer."[2]

Of the many artists' studios I have seen, Van Nice's working space is memorable because it afforded me insight into her working methods and creative processes. Through endless improvisation, informed associations, and exquisite craftsmanship, she makes order out of chaos. On one particular visit, I was free for a day to explore her space unaccompanied, and I experienced a true wonderland where both Lewis Carroll's Alice and Marcel Duchamp would feel right at home. In Van Nice's enormous studio, detritus scoured from the streets of Somerville on garbage day underwent a process of poetic transformation. Broken lamp stands became long-necked cranes, pages from Nicolas Shakespeare's biography of Bruce Chatwin were cut into strips and turned into a broom, and used books were altered and "served up" as part of a luxurious meal in Van Nice's brilliant book installation *Dinner with Mr. Dewey* (pp. 187–89). It was nothing short of magical, and I was glad that, through *The Book as Art* exhibitions, the museum was bringing a taste of that magic to our visitors.

In addition to visiting artists all over the world and welcoming those who came to Washington, D.C., I have also made an effort to see major collections of artists' books at home and abroad. Naturally, some of these visits resulted in the acquisition of exciting new works. Thanks to Sylvie Alix, curator of special collections at the Bibliothèque Nationale du Québec in Montreal, I was able to examine and subsequently purchase a copy of Brenda Watson's *Comment attirer les oiseaux?* (pp. 54–55), a whimsical book with wing-shaped pages. Among private collections, the Ruth and Marvin Sackner Archives of Concrete and Visual Poetry in Miami, Florida, has been a source of continual revelation and several acquisitions, including *Unfinished Symphony* by Elena Presser (p. 168).

In my experience as a librarian and book arts curator I was often surprised by the great originality and beauty of works created by completely unknown artists. While I was delighted to acquire works by such famous and established artists as May Stevens, Meret Oppenheim, and Kara Walker, I was also impressed by the virtuosity of many artists working in obscurity. It is a pleasure to bring the gifts of these artists to the attention of the world beyond the community of book artists, collectors, publishers, librarians, curators, and rare book dealers.

This volume was designed to showcase the artists' books collection at the National Museum of Women in the Arts, to spark the imagination of readers, and to broaden popular understanding of and appreciation for this art form. It seeks to whet the appetites of potential new collectors and to inspire budding artists to try their hands at creating artists' books. Its organization proposes not to divide artists' books into formal categories but to unite them, in all their manifestations of structure, contents, and material.

The artists' books are grouped into nine thematic sections, each containing examples of the major categories of artists' books from unique books to multiple bookworks. The first of these is *Storytellers*. Women all over the world and in every age have delighted in sharing tales with other women, with friends and relations, and

Storytellers

Donatella Franchi (Italian, b. 1942)

The Legacy of Scheherazade, 2002

Ink and watercolor on rice paper

60 x 48 in.

Unique artist's book

Gift of June Rosner

"Every woman who is a storyteller is a Scheherazade," said Moroccan writer Fatema Mernissi, describing her grandmother Jasmina. Illiterate, Jasmina heard the stories of Scheherazade, the narrator of *1,001 Arabian Nights*, told by other women, and she knew them by heart. Sometimes the teller would adapt the story to convey her own message. This is what Jasmina did with her favorite tale, "The Story of Hassan al-Basri." She called it "The Woman with the Feather Dress." The story takes place in Baghdad, where Hassan, an attractive young man, is watching the sea from a terrace. Suddenly a big bird lands on the seashore, gracefully sheds its plumage, and a naked woman of amazing beauty appears. While she is bathing in the sea, Hassan, crazy with love, hides her feather dress in a secret place. The woman, now without wings, must agree to marry him. They live quite happily together for several years, but one day the woman finds her feather dress—for which she has never stopped searching—and flies away with her two children.

The original version of the story has a different ending: Hassan crosses the seas and finds his wife and children. In Jasmina's version, Hassan spends the rest of his life looking for them. The message Jasmina wanted to convey was about freedom: a woman should always defend her freedom, even when she is loved.

For me, this is the legacy of Scheherazade, the storyteller who overcomes the sultan's destructive impulses and changes him into a loving man through her belief in life and the power of words.

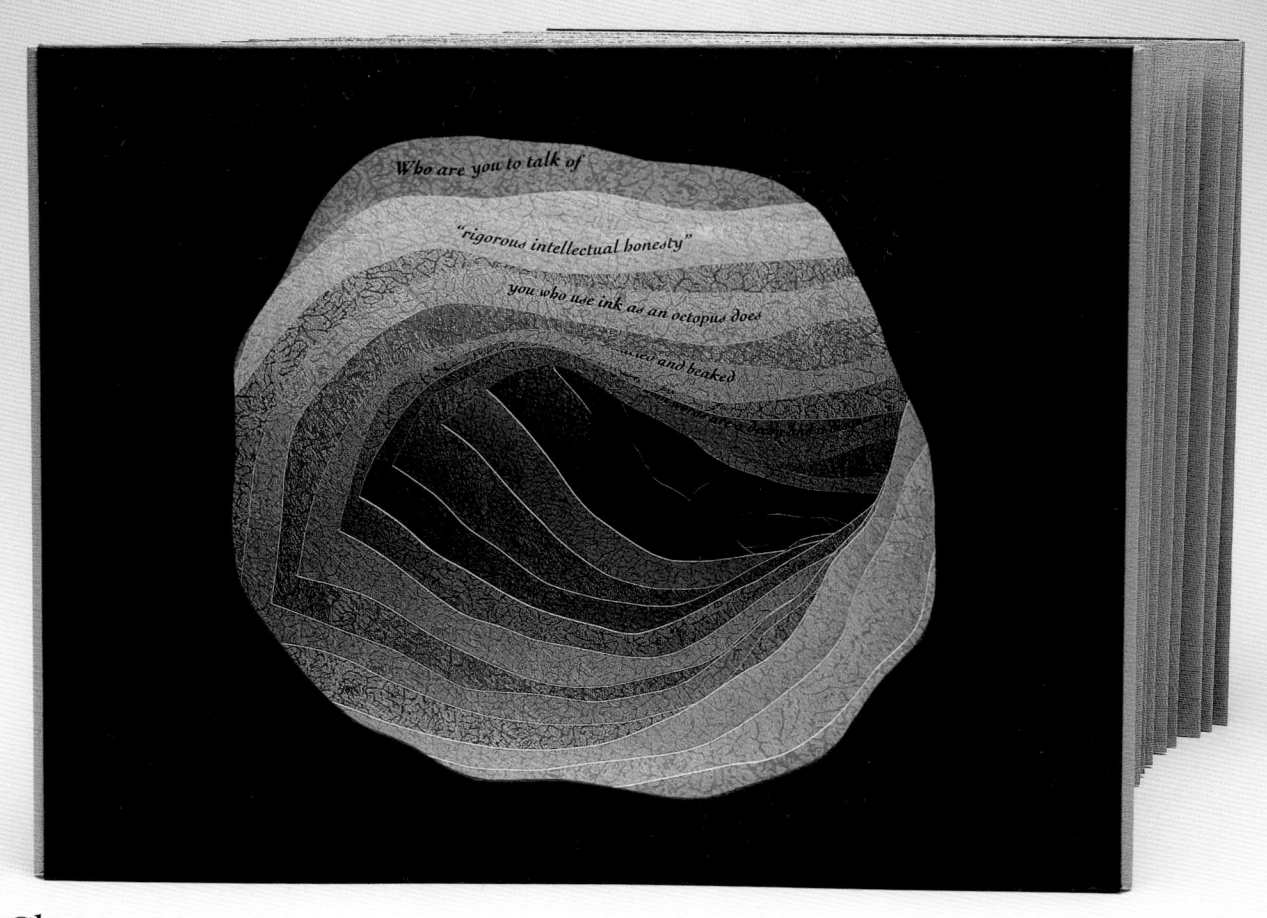

Julie Chen (American, b. 1963)

Octopus, 1992

Poem by Elizabeth McDevitt

Letterpress on paper

13.5 x 10.75 in.

Edition of 100; Flying Fish Press, Berkeley, California

Gift of United States Department of Education

"Octopus" is a poem about loss and, to a lesser extent, about language. The central irony of the poem is that language, normally a means of connecting people, here creates distance. The book's tunnel structure is a three-dimensional space that suggests the shadowy undersea world of the octopus, the main figure in the poem. The octopus represents "the other" in a troubled relationship, disappearing behind a screen of words that confuse rather than clarify the speaker's understanding of the relationship. Because the tunnel format provides a three-dimensional experience of perspective and distance, it illustrates the idea of a thing receding, growing distant, and finally disappearing. The viewer's experience reading lines that grow progressively farther away is meant to mirror the speaker's difficulty interpreting the language of the other, as well as to underscore the speaker's growing sense of isolation and loss at the end of the poem.

*T*rue to Life is about the subtle yet powerful influence that memory has on daily life. Personal history, while seemingly rooted in fact, may contain more meaning as narrative than as documentation of truth. The inspiration for this piece came from observing my own process of remembering difficult episodes from my life. Memories of specific events would come to mind at unexpected moments with painful clarity. As this process continued over a period of several months, I began to notice that what had started out seeming like a solid accounting of the facts was, in fact, subtly changing over time.

I wanted the physical structure of the book to express the shifting nature of memory in order to give the reader a deeper understanding of the ideas presented in the text. In the form of a tablet with sliding pages, *True to Life* allows the reader to create different combinations of text and image and thus alter the content of the piece, deliberately or by chance, with each reading.

Julie Chen (American, b. 1963)

True to Life, 2004

Letterpress printed using a combination of pressure plates, woodblocks, photopolymer plates, Plexiglas, wood

10 x 15 x 2.5 in.

Edition of 100; Flying Fish Press, Berkeley, California

Anonymous gift

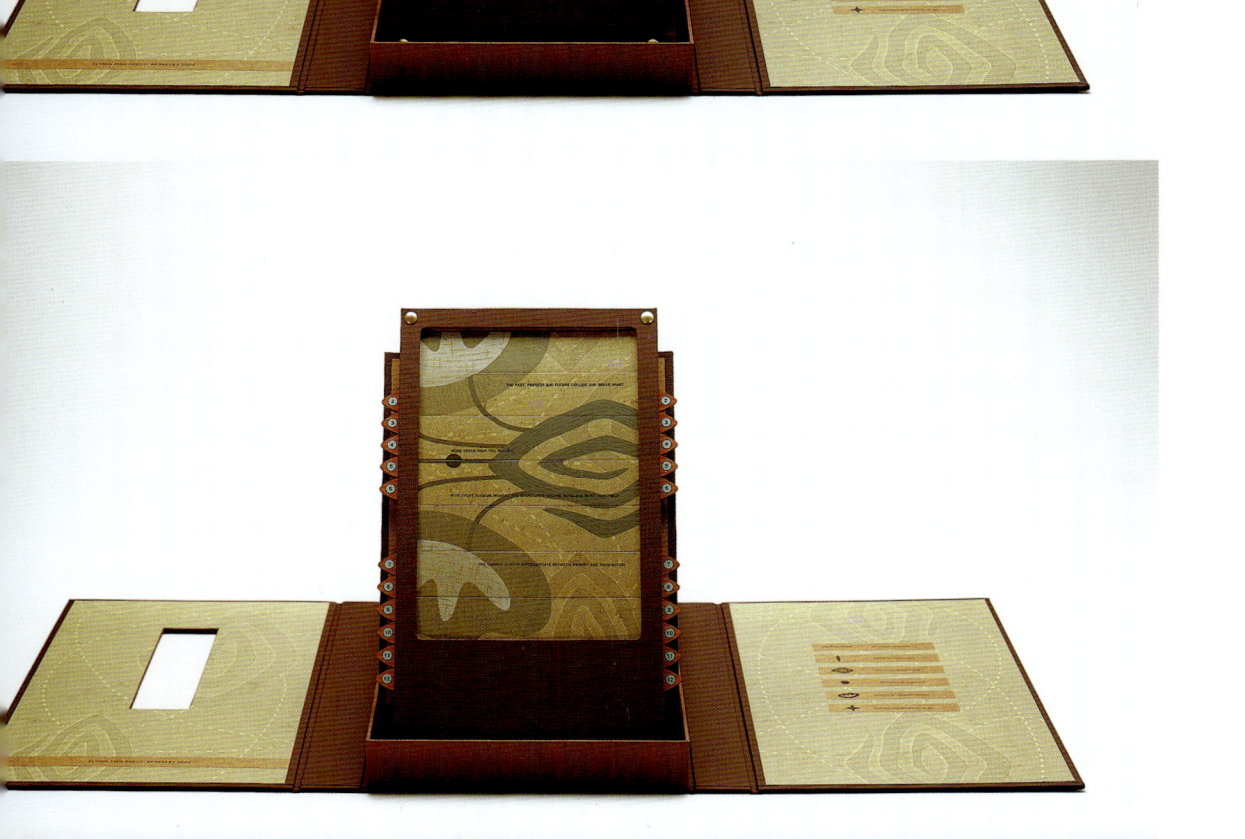

Vera Khlebnikova (Russian, b. 1954)

Woman concerned in art, having a flat, a child, had made this book of newspaper's ads. About myself: living in Moscow, Taurus, 50/172/80, D&D free, non-smkr. Vera Khlebnikova., 2005

Screenprint on paper and canvas

13.5 x 18 in.

Edition of 125; Hand Print Workshop International, Alexandria, Virginia

Gift of NMWA Library Fellows

Under Communist rule, all Soviet newspapers passed through strict censors, and reproducing or photocopying text was prohibited. In the 1990s, during the economic, political, and social reform of *perestroika* and *glasnost*, censorship was abolished. Suddenly magazines and newspapers began to publish personal advertisements, and soon entire newspapers dedicated themselves to printing ads, unedited and free of charge. Most of the ads concerned items for sale, people seeking spouses or companions, or the availability of sexual services.

Then special sections titled "Messages" began to appear. They were very short, and they invited embellishment in the mind of the reader. One still makes my skin cold: "I die leaving a four-year-old daughter, wonderful girl. Caring, loving each other, childless foster parents are sought. 184291, Murmansk region, Revda." I clipped this advertisement for no reason I could name. Then I added others, but they all felt incomplete: I needed faces. I wanted to see the people who wrote these terrible, funny, crazy messages. I own hundreds of old photos of people no one can identify. To make this book, I matched the people in the photographs to the stories suggested by the advertisements I had clipped.

is for Gina
smiling
all day

Ovubet is deliberately both delicate and disturbing—a deceptively simple execution of a complicated subject. It documents the early sexual awakening of twenty-six fictional girls by examining stifled childhood habits and feelings of adolescent vulnerability. Rendering the progress of innocence into awareness, this work chronicles the beauty of awkward girlhood moments. We are captivated by the resilience of our own virgin selves and beguiled by the lure of shameless sensuality. *Ovubet* is a dictionary of intimate scenarios, inviting viewers to observe without fear of trespassing or offending.

The oval doilies used in the piece were tested by a conservator and found to be so impregnated with plastic that they would last longer than acid-free paper. I collaborated with Jack Lemon on the etchings, then hand-colored each myself. Lemon and I designed a candy box containing a candy map that acts as an introduction to the set.

Peregrine Honig (American, b. 1976)

Ovubet (26 Girls with Sweet Centers), 1999

Drypoint etching and watercolor on paper doilies

7.5 x 10 in.

Edition of 20; Landfall Press, Chicago

Gift of Lois Pollard Price

Joyce Ellen Weinstein (American, b. 1940)

Birds Head Haggadah, 1998

Parchment, watercolor, ink, leather, brass, beads, velvet

8.5 x 9.5 in.

Unique artist's book

Gift of the artist

Throughout history Jews have been called the People of the Book; this work is a reflection of that identity. The original *Birds Head Haggadah*, a book of prayer from southern Germany circa 1300, curiously depicts humans with the heads of birds. One theory suggests that the artist avoided painting human faces in obeisance of a Jewish law banning graven images.

My own *Birds Head Haggadah* combines photographs, photocopies, and found objects with abstract forms, color, and drawings to create an object that appears unstable and mysterious, as if it were an artifact from another time and place. The hammered brass *repoussé* cover is made to look like an ancient Bible, a found treasure. *Birds Head Haggadah* comments on the act of remembering; memories are nothing more than hints about the past and are neither concrete nor absolute.

I might suddenly have felt the urge to harm her, and easily could've. But of course that was not my thought. She turned back to the door and seemed to hurry her key into the lock. She looked my way once more, as I heard the bolt shoot profoundly back. I said nothing, did not even look at her again. I didn't want her to think my mind contained what it did and also what it did not.

And I walked on then, feeling oddly but in no way surprisingly betrayed, simply passed on down the street toward my room and my own doors, my life entering, as it was at that moment, its first long cycle of necessity.

"Privacy" is the story of a man who, unable to sleep, stands wrapped in a blanket looking out his apartment window. He sees, and perhaps is also seen. He spends several nights watching a woman undress in a distant window, until through a chance daytime encounter he discovers that she is much older than he believed. Eventually, he returns to the privacy of the bed he shares with his wife.

In creating the companion images to Richard Ford's story, I read and drew, developing form through repetition and mutation. It took many readings and many drawings to find a pictorial logic that was consonant with the format of the text. Repetitious images of eyes allude to the voyeuristic inclinations of the protagonist, and the darker pages suggest the atmosphere of night. I did a structural mock-up in gouache and then worked with the master printer Jennifer Melby to make the seven sheets that, when folded, make fourteen pages with text printed in letterpress directly on top of the etchings.

Jane Kent (American, b. 1952)

Privacy, 1999

Story by Richard Ford

Etching and letterpress on paper

10.5 x 15.25 in.

Edition of 35; The Grenfell Press, New York

Gift of Lois Pollard Price

GLOVE STORY
PAT OLESZKO

My work as a performance artist utilizes many media, yet has remained somewhat ephemeral, if not altogether fleeting. Looking for new vistas to augment that peripatetic life, I faced the challenge of creating something other than the fragile moment/memory of a time-based performance. A book was one solution. *Glove Story* is a performance for the lap. It exhibits the eye and hand of the artist, yet remains available, reliable, and never needs feeding.

The text is a play, a ploy, a costume drama, and a pun-ridden metaphorical plow through contemporary personal relations. The text introduces Ms. Glove Lee, a gossip columnist who dispenses spare but pungent advice to her weakly readers. Letters arrive from characteristically adorned gloves, inhabitants of a world where the paper is the *Hand Me Down News* and the denizens affect revealing monikers, such as Tee He, Rolf D' Cuff, and Three Finger Tham. The queries range from the immeasurable demands of Juan Ruler to the artists' color quandary of Rainbow Hugh. Glove Lee answers all, tongue firmly planted in cheek, in terse prose and cons. Eventually in the course of her professional generosity, Glove Lee finds and advises a certain Lone Lee. They meet, and it is, of course, glove at first sight, all of which amounts to handling a torrid tale with kid gloves.

Pat Oleszko (American, b. 1947)

Glove Story, 1996

Lithography, scanned photographs, linen, cotton gloves

15.5 x 15.5 in.

Edition of 50; Landfall Press, Chicago

Gift of United States Department of Education

Originally *Residue* was created as an experimental installation piece for a one-night art event in a hotel. Using a hotel room with its minimal furnishings as the basis of the piece, I collaborated with poet Susan Weiner to address a social issue that is a common occurrence within such an environment. *Residue* is about human connection and disconnection in the context of an affair. The viewer was invited to explore a visual treatment of the poem's text, from the first verse embroidered on the top bed sheet, to the second verse installed on the shower stall walls using human hair, and so on.

Inspired by the response and our collaboration, *Residue* was re-created in book form. It is constructed in the sculptural form of a bed with sheets and two pillows without cases. The bed has to be turned down before the book can be opened. The pages are pillowcases with embroidered text; the viewer has to unfold each pillowcase to read the poetry and then refold it to continue. The task of unfolding and refolding is a metaphor for the disruption created by entering into a love affair and the "remaking" required to exit from it. The work addresses the existential human condition of being alone even as we struggle to connect.

Rosemarie Chiarlone (American, b. 1951)

Residue, 2003

Poem by Susan Weiner

Pillowcases, pillows, thread

17 x 30 in.

Edition of 3; published by the artist, Miami, Florida

Gift of Lorraine Grace

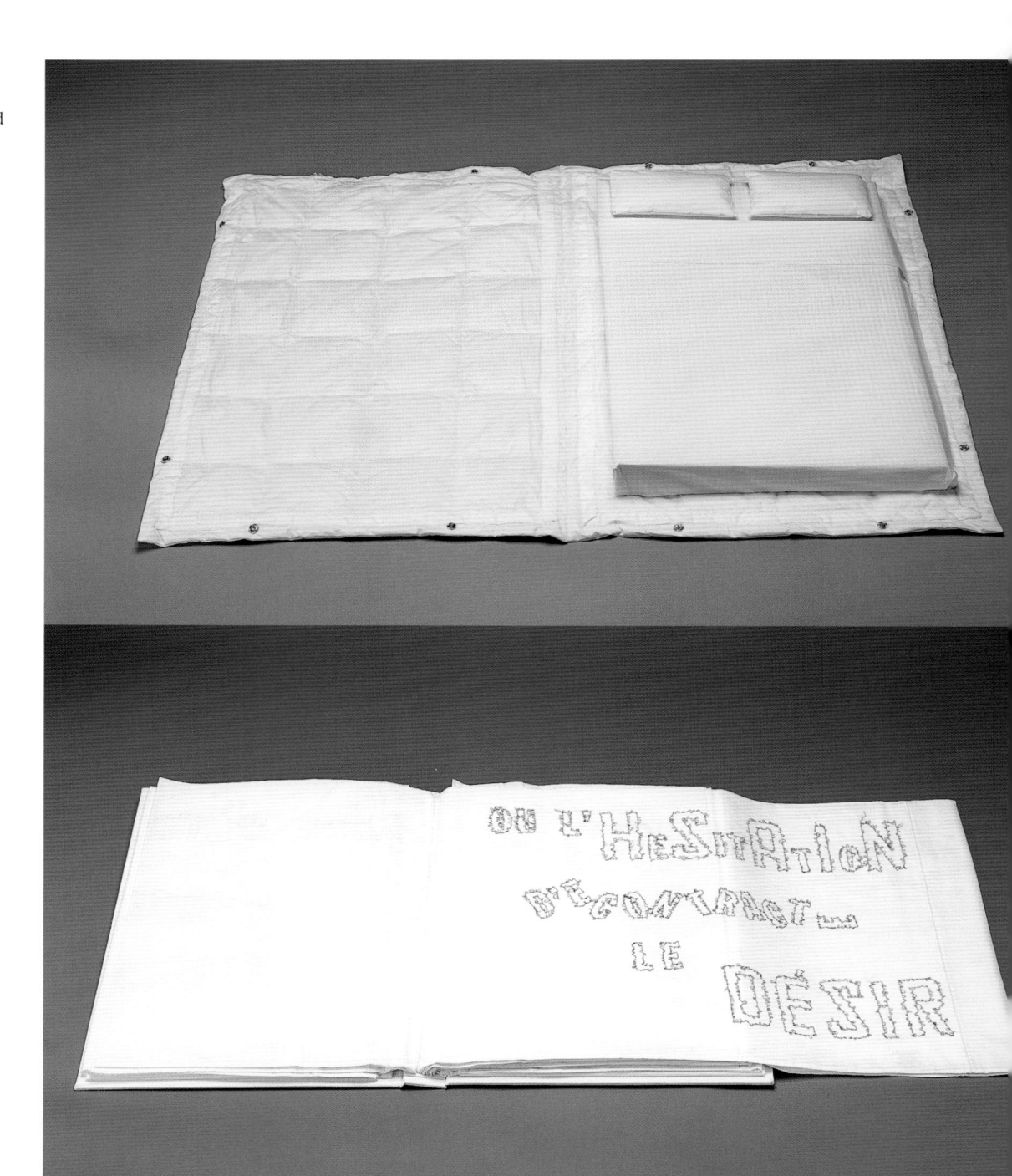

Kumi Korf (American, b. Japan, 1937)

Silk and Secrecy, 1985

Story by Emoretta Yang

Photo offset on paper, silk thread, Japanese paper scrolls

11.5 x 15.5 in.

Edition of 20; published by the artist, Ithaca, New York

Gift of the artist

I have memories of my great-aunt's rearing of silkworms, processing the cocoons and turning them into thread, and then weaving the threads into fabric. My conversations with Emoretta Yang about the alchemy of silk gave us the idea for this book. The secrecy surrounding the culture of silkworms and the production of silk inspired Emoretta to write this allegorical story about a young silk worker's deadly fall into the depths of a mystical silk forest. The worker is overcome by the trees' power to extract confessions, and he unravels all of his secrets, including his illicit relationship with the beautiful wife of a silk merchant. The story links the process of winding silk threads with hiding and telling secrets.

I created a group of small scrolls wound with colorful silk threads. The scrolls bear silk-related images, partly visible between the binding threads. To present the concept of secrecy in a concrete manner, the scrolls had to be bound and inaccessible. If one reaches to open a scroll, it forces the destruction not only of the object but also of the carefully guarded secrets.

Kara Walker uses the Victorian medium of the silhouette to relate stories about slavery and its continuing legacy in American society. *Freedom* describes the imaginary sea journey of a small group of recently emancipated slaves heading to an uncertain destination. Walker's alter ego, the nineteenth-century "Negress," struggles with her identity as she naively contemplates the color of her skin, her insidious relationship with her master, and her fantasies of Africa as a safe haven. Like most of the artist's narratives, the tale addresses the sexually and psychologically violent history of race relations in America. Using antique fonts and imagery, Walker captures the fog-covered, oppressive atmosphere of the postwar South.

Kara Walker (American b. 1969)

Freedom: A Fable; A Curious Interpretation of the Wit of a Negress in Troubled Times, with Illustrations, 1997

Paper, leather

8.25 x 9.5 in.

Edition of 4,000; The Peter Norton Family Christmas Project,

Santa Monica, California

Gift of Marla Prather

Angela Lorenz (American, b. 1965)
Soap Story, 1999

Linen, soap, acid-free paper, book cloth, cardboard

Box: 6.25 x 4.5 x 1 in.; book: 5.75 x 4 in.; soap cube: 1.5 x 1.5 x 1.5 in.

Edition of 200; published by the artist, Bologna, Italy

Gift of Lois Pollard Price

Soap Story tells the tale of a young woman in 1950s Calabria, Italy, whose life reads like a rags-to-riches fairy tale or a soap opera in six installments. The protagonist is an unwed mother, ostracized and barred entry to the only place for doing laundry in her tiny town. A doctor, who is also unmarried, moves to the town and hires the woman to wash and cook for him. They soon fall in love, marry, and have children. The doctor's wife becomes the richest woman in town, with all of her troubles washed away.

The reader must release the text, which is silkscreened on linen pages, from six tiny bars of soap with numbers imprinted on them with lead type. After they are hung to dry (ironing optional), the rags fit into six acid-free pages with oval die-cuts, through which the text remains visible. The process confronting the reader is the same as that of the protagonist. She must transform her story and wash her hands of her sorrows.

Renée Stout (American, b. 1958)

Seven Windows, 1996

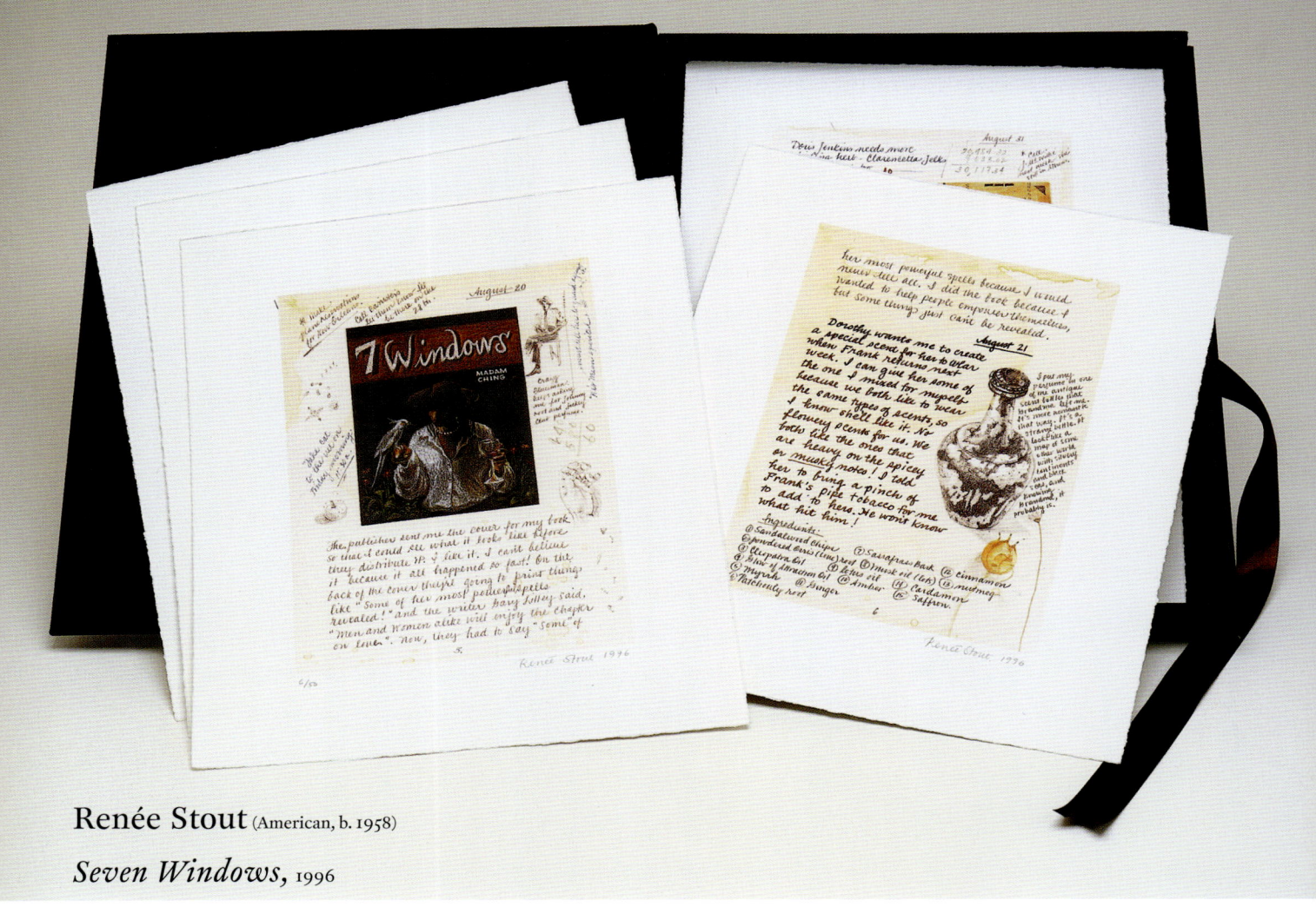

Iris prints on paper

10 x 12 in.

Edition of 50; David Adamson Gallery, Washington, D.C.

Gift of United States Department of Education

In creating *Seven Windows*, my desire was to allow the viewer a glimpse into the world of Madam Ching, who was once an alter ego of mine. Madam Ching, a mysterious fortuneteller and root worker, functioned as a vehicle through which I could analyze the complexities of the self and human relationships. Set up in the form of nine pages from a journal, *Seven Windows* situates the viewer as voyeur, following the daily activities of Madam Ching as she brews perfumes and love potions, buys and sells exotic herbs and ingredients, and reads letters from friends and lovers. The journal pages are accompanied by tiny drawings, stamps, and cigar labels. The title comes from the fact that the studio where I was living and working at the time the piece was created had seven large windows that gave me an expansive view of the street and the neighborhood from which much of my inspiration was drawn.

Nature

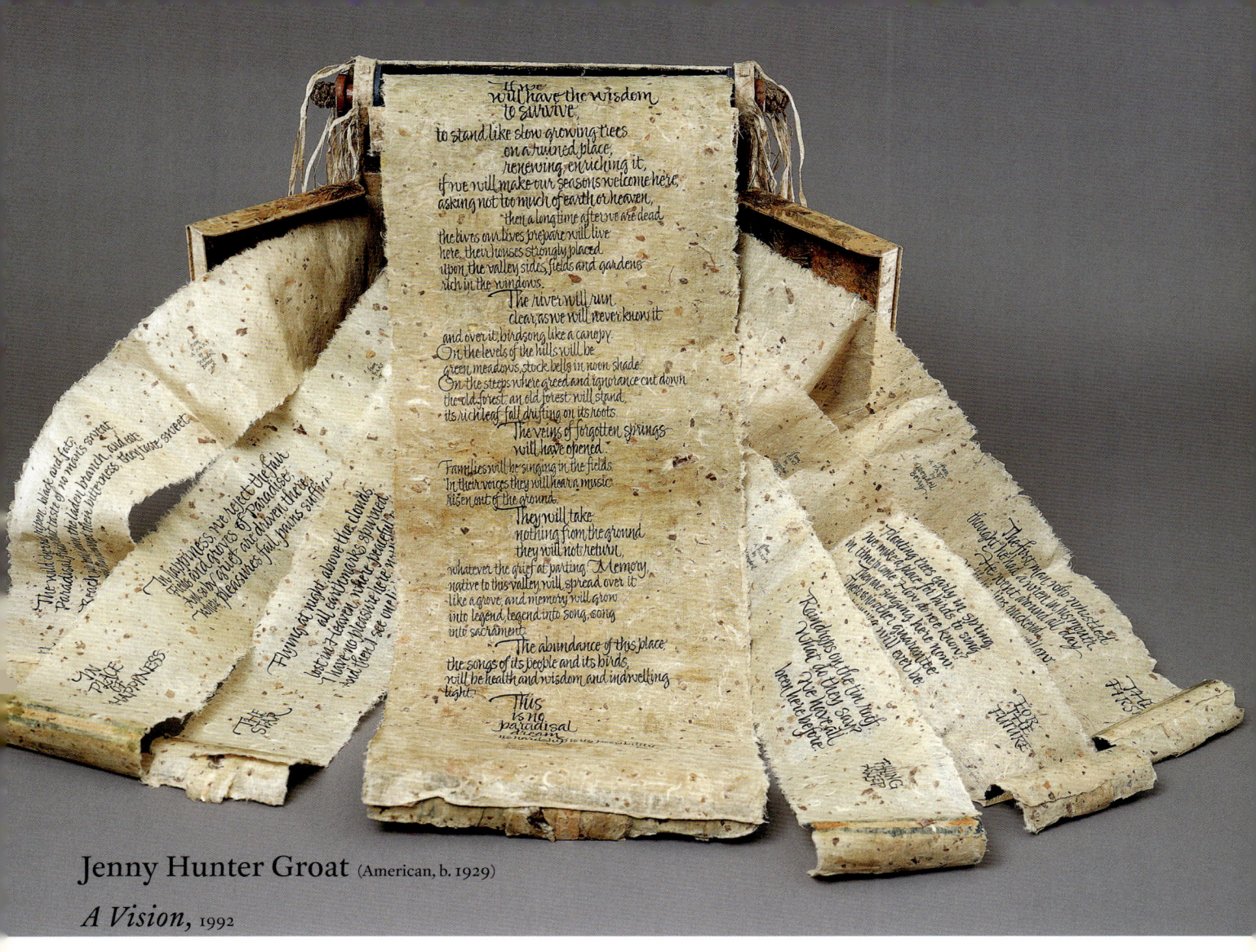

Jenny Hunter Groat (American, b. 1929)
A Vision, 1992

Poems by Wendell Berry

Mat board, Chinese paper, Japanese tea chest paper, linen threads, seed cones, wood bark, plants of the redwood forest

12 x 9 x 3.25 in.

Unique artist's book

Gift of NMWA Library Fellows

"This wonderful house...you have made for my poems," wrote poet Wendell Berry on receiving photos of *A Vision*. I love the poetry and essays of Berry, who writes of wilderness and simplicity, and I wanted to create a book that would unfold to the richness of his words. In my concept, the nonverbal structure prepares the reader for the words it contains. I was a dancer and choreographer, and for me the *movement* toward the final scroll is the important thing about the book's form. I constructed the cabinet and, except for the structural materials, everything I used was gathered from the natural flora surrounding my home.

I chose six short poems from the collection *A Part* to become the smaller scrolls and the poem "A Vision," from *Clearing*, to be the final unfolding scroll. These poems reflect my own feelings about nature. While focusing on the vulnerability of the environment, I now include the joy and overriding victory that the energies of nature, properly understood, will always have, with or without humans. I find this idea full of hope since I, too, am nature.

Suburban sprawl, population density, and the loss of undeveloped land are themes that inspired me to create the magnetic book *RIM*. Starting at the edge of the city of Detroit and progressing outward twelve miles, I asked residents to respond anonymously to a survey about the location of their home and the things they liked about it. I mounted the responses on top of a rural landscape painting. The book slides open to form a circle with a hollow core, representing the fate of inner cities when sprawl is allowed to continue unabated.

Susan Goethel Campbell (American, b. 1956)

RIM, 2000

Mixed media, magnetic sheeting

8 x 3 x 2 in.

Edition of 6; published by the artist, Huntington Woods, Michigan

NMWA Members' Art Acquisition Fund

Susan Goethel Campbell (American, b. 1956)

After the Deluge, 2002

Photoetching with aquatint and chine collé on Japanese paper, letterpress printed from photopolymer plates

11 x 14 in.

Edition of 10; published by the artist, Huntington Woods, Michigan

NMWA Members' Art Acquisition Fund

Loosely based on the biblical story of Noah's ark, *After the Deluge* tells the stories, both comic and tragic, of various animal species and how they are faring in the early twenty-first century. The narrative and the sixteen photoetchings in the book are based on newspaper articles collected from the *New York Times* and the *Detroit Free Press* that document human encroachment on animal habitats. The book is encased in a faux-leather folder with a magnetic closure resembling the astronomical constellation Columba, "the dove," and inside are alphabetized names of animal species that float across the interior flaps like constellations in the night sky. The binding and folder were designed in collaboration with Daniel Kelm.

Brenda Watson (Canadian, b. 1964)

Comment attirer les oiseaux?

(How to attract birds?), 1995

Oil paint on aluminum, rubber, thread

30 x 10 in.

Edition of 12; published by the artist, Montreal, Canada

NMWA Library and Research Center Book Acquisition Fund

Comment attirer les oiseaux? reflects on the intrinsic value of the wild spirit. The title implies the human desire to tame wild things, be they animals, landscapes, or other people.

One of the things that attracts us to birds is their ability to fly; to people, flight is a metaphor for freedom. Yet we put birds in cages so they can't fly away. The reasons for birds' flight—to find food, a mate, shelter; to avoid danger; and to migrate—are as immutable as the reasons for our own daily displacements. Without choice there is no freedom.

The physical shape of the book is significant in that birds have the ability to travel between the urban and the natural worlds. The birds depicted in the book are found in the area surrounding the small logging, mining, and farming community in which I grew up, echoing my own migration from a rural to an urban life.

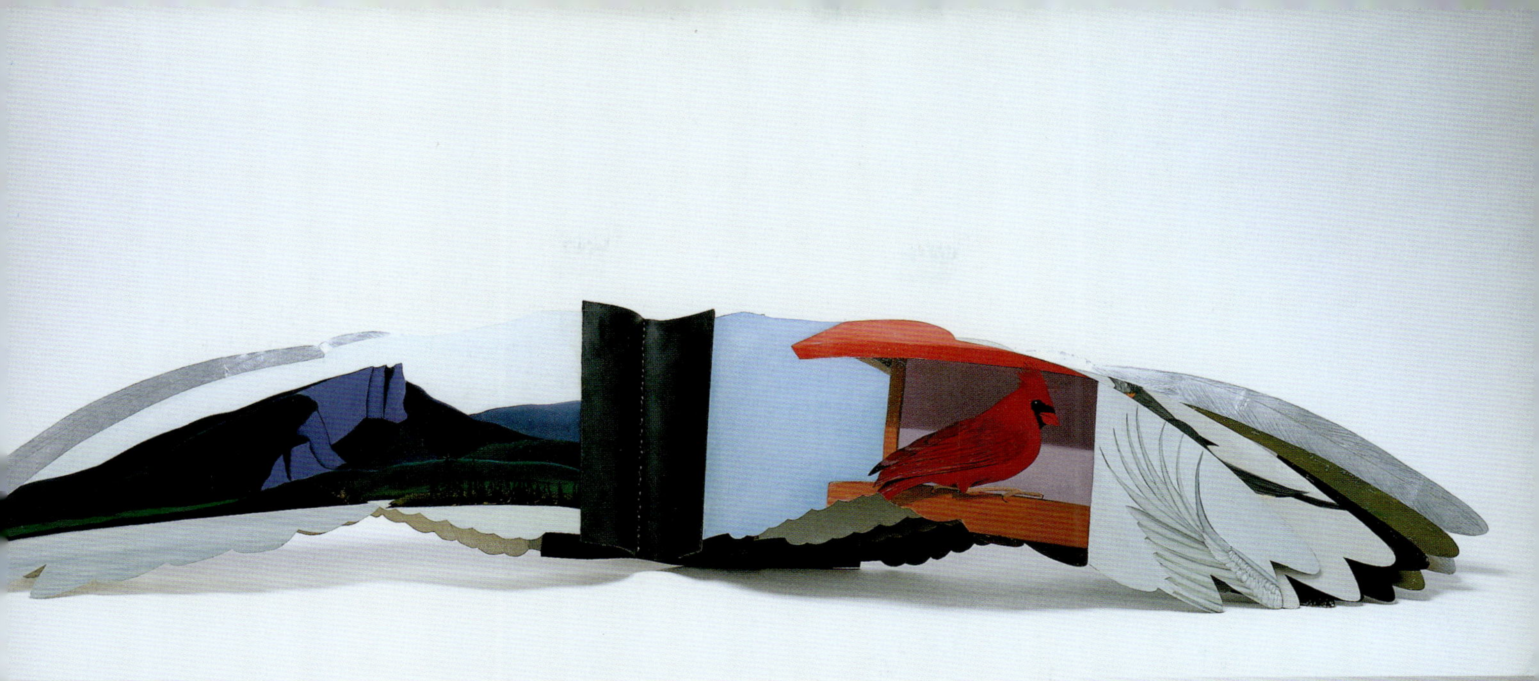

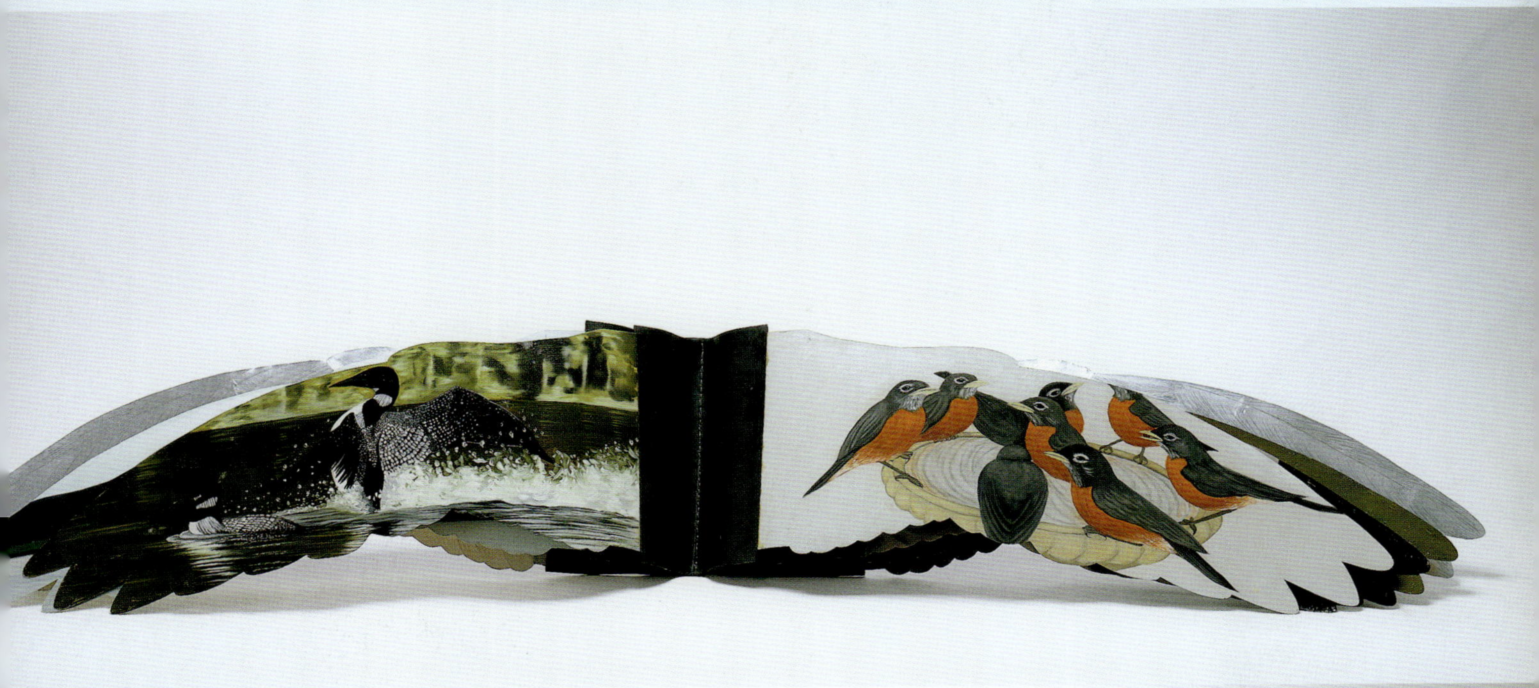

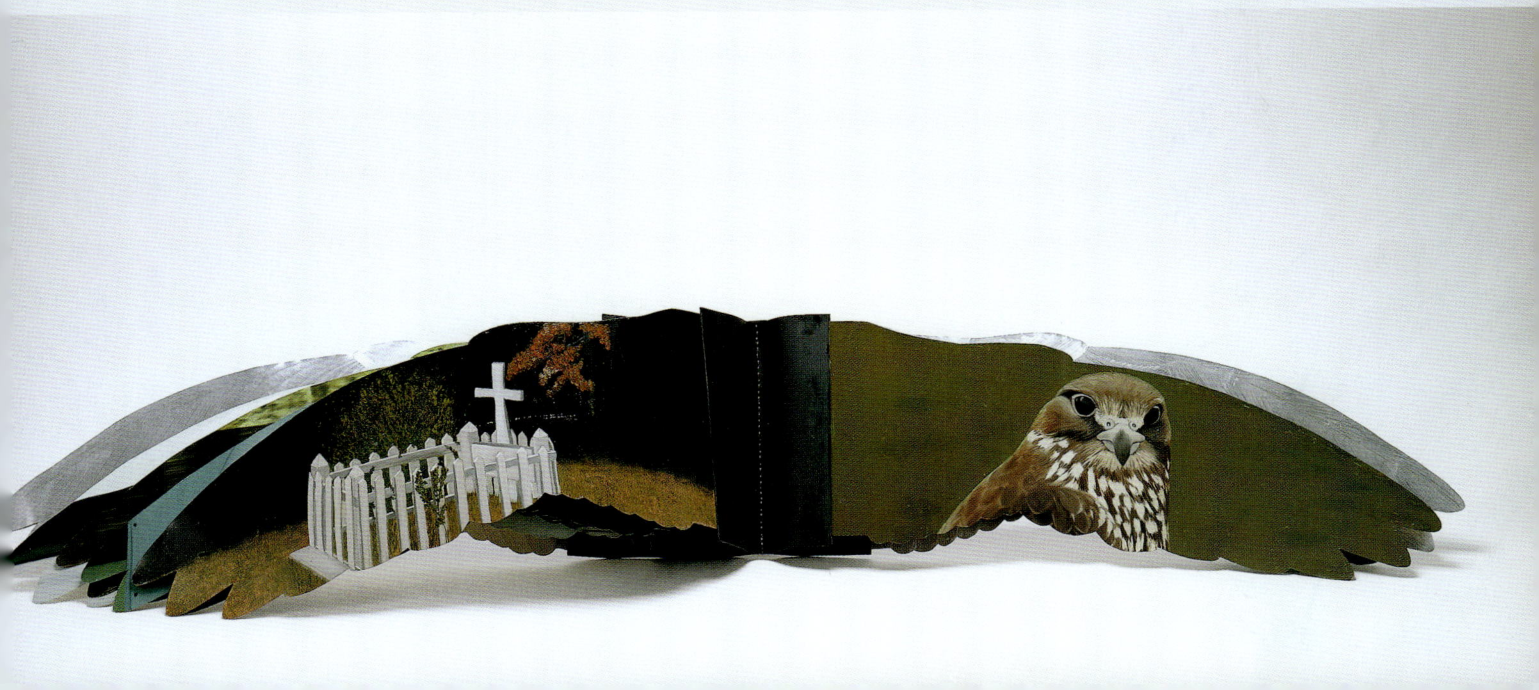

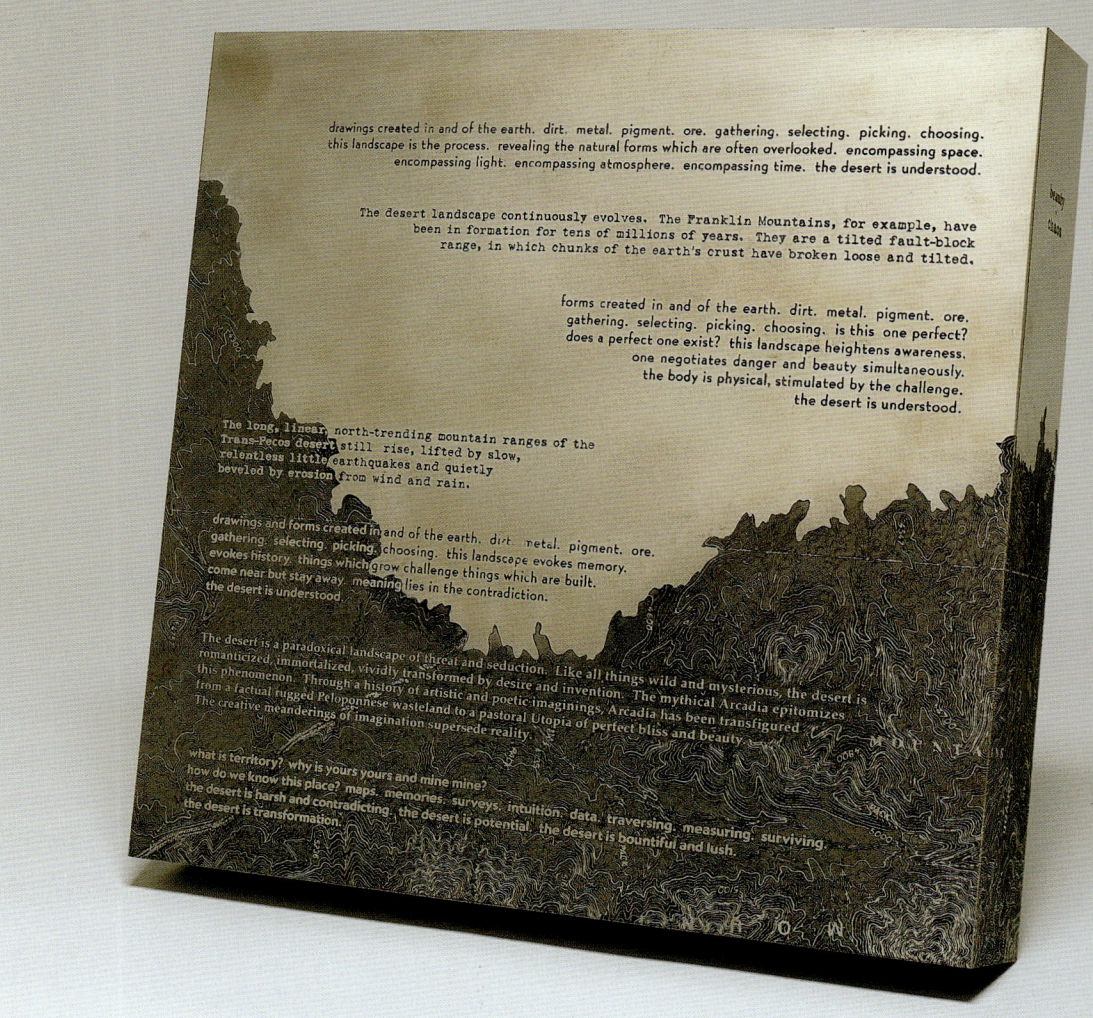

Susan Davidoff (American, b. 1953)

Beverly Penn (American, b. 1955)

Rachelle Thiewes (American, b. 1952)

Beauty.Chaos, 1999

Charcoal drawings, etching, slate, nickel, silver

11 x 10.75 x 2 in.

Edition of 6; published by the artists, El Paso, Texas

Gift of NMWA Texas State Committee

Landscape in general, and the high Chihuahuan Desert of west Texas in particular, have played a pivotal role in shaping the way the three of us approach our individual work as artists. Although we work in different media, we share a strong interest in the desert, the land, and the way people interact with their environments. In 1999 we formally explored these connections in a collaborative series of books titled *Beauty.Chaos*. In each book, we presented collections of drawn images, sculptural objects, and texts that were a visual reflection of the many journeys we had taken together the previous year.

The journey through this volume begins with the book's metal jacket sleeve, created by Beverly Penn, which is etched with a topographic map of the landscape we explored and inscriptions of our thoughts during the collaboration. Slipping the book from its metal sleeve, one opens the silk casing to reveal Rachelle Thiewes' small sculpture in metal and slate, suggestive of a cactus thorn, which reflects both the seductive and threatening botanical forms of the desert and the light that sustains them. Lifting an adjacent overleaf, the viewer discovers Susan Davidoff's series of drawings, created in charcoal and natural pigments taken from the desert itself. Through these diverse and unusual materials, *Beauty.Chaos* explores patterns, layers, and the complexities and contradictions of the Chihuahuan Desert.

Elisabetta Gut (Italian, b. 1934)

Libro-seme (Seed-book), 1983

Seed shell, paper pages

5 x 4 x 4 in.

Unique book-object

Gift of the artist

For my first "seed-book," made in 1979, the poetic idea came to me as I opened and closed my hands, in which I held two shells of some exotic fruit. I envisioned the shells as the cover of a book. I took sheets of rice paper with Japanese ideograms, cut them in the shape of the shells, and bound them. The first impression was amazing— I had created a book different in shape and content—an offering to both nature and culture. This *Libro-seme* is very similar, although I replaced the ideograms with sheet music. The notes represent seeds, from which culture grows and blossoms.

For thousands of years the snake has been a powerful and magical symbol in many cultures and is often associated with women, both positively and negatively. Whether representing good or evil, creation or destruction, the source of life or the advent of death, the snake has a hypnotic hold on our collective imagination. My research into the lives of these creatures provided the basis for the descriptive poem that accompanies the imagery. The forms were inspired by my travels to view the works of artists in India, Japan, Australia, Africa, Brazil, northwest Canada, and Alaska.

Betty R. Sweren (American, b. 1931)

The Snake, 1995

Pulp painting with color pigment and mica on handmade paper

10 x 9.5 in.

Edition of 30; published by the artist, Baltimore, Maryland

Gift of the artist

Inspired by travel to the southwestern desert, I created a series of six hand-lettered and painted books titled *The Desert Speaks*. Each book contains text by Edward Abbey focusing on a different aspect of life in the desert landscape. In Book One, Abbey's text invites the reader to consider the importance of wilderness to our culture, not only for its beauty but for its offer of solitude. The washes of color, words, and symbols evoke blue mesas, red rock canyons, and distant snow-covered peaks.

Nancy Leavitt (American, b. 1953)

The Desert Speaks, Book One, 1992

Text by Edward Abbey

Watercolor and gouache on paper, woven cotton, raw silk

4.63 x 12.13 in.

Unique artist's book

Gift of Lois Pollard Price

Sas Colby (American, b. 1939)

Stones of Sorrow, 1991

Canvas, stones, thread, paint

12 x 12 in.

Unique artist's book

Gift of Coille Hooven

Stones of Sorrow is from a series of painted canvas books created in Taos, New Mexico, between 1990 and 1995. This book emerged from a collection of beach stones arranged as talismans to illustrate familiar aphorisms. Stones are considered inanimate, but to me they are alive: they are objects of wonder, possessing magical qualities. I can't resist holding them and sensing their mysteries.

The stones deployed on these pages invite touch. They also emphasize the repetitious cadence of the word "stone," giving each page a heaviness that makes it plop down while stone tabs provide a standard for turning the pages. Cut-out voids lead the viewer through to the final page: the last stone, the gravestone.

Food and the Body

Allison Cooke Brown (American, b. 1950)

Teatimes, 2005

Teabags, sepia ink, silk-covered box with paper lining, bone clasp

5.75 x 5.75 x 3 in.

Unique artist's book

Gift of Wilhelmina Cole Holladay

In *Teatimes*, I record my daily ritual of pouring a cup of tea and writing in my journal. From a case that replicates a Salada tea box, the reader selects and unfolds an empty tea bag and discovers a fragment of a journal entry. Where once there were tea leaves, now there are reflections written in sepia ink. There is a distinct contrast between the bags' exteriors, with their bright red commercial labels and declarative statements, and the unwrapped interiors, with handwritten personal musings. Private thoughts are steeping.

63

Susan Joy Share (American, b. 1954)

Carrots Anyone? 1999

Board, paper, cloth, photocopy, Styrofoam

13 x 11 x .75 in.

Unique artist's book

NMWA Library and Research Center Book Acquisition Fund

Carrots Anyone? reflects on the mixed messages we receive from the food industry in its simultaneous effort to entice us and to pander to our obsession with body weight. It is a wearable component of a performance piece in which the carrot books are sold the way sensual "cigarette girls" once offered their wares in dance halls. The text in the book includes phrases such as "big on taste," "low in fat," "look and feel good," "satisfying," "all natural," and "think thin."

In the 1960s, before "the personal is political" became a mantra, I felt as though I was out on a limb dealing with subject matter we would now call feminist. Later, as feminism emerged and autobiographical elements were increasingly accepted in art, I struggled with how to use personal events in my work. I was not interested in self-revelation but in striking a note of common experience. Many women will relate to *The Gynecologist*, in which a male physician attempts to persuade his patient to have a hysterectomy. His lack of true understanding about women's minds and bodies quickly becomes apparent. Patient-doctor interviews like the one recorded in this book are still all too common. In my research I was led through dense texts and startling statistics to these ancient representations of the female reproductive system dating from the fourteenth to the eighteenth centuries.

Joan Lyons (American, b. 1937)

The Gynecologist, 1989

Offset on paper

6 x 9 in.

Edition of 1,000; Visual Studies Workshop Press, Rochester, New York

Gift of the artist

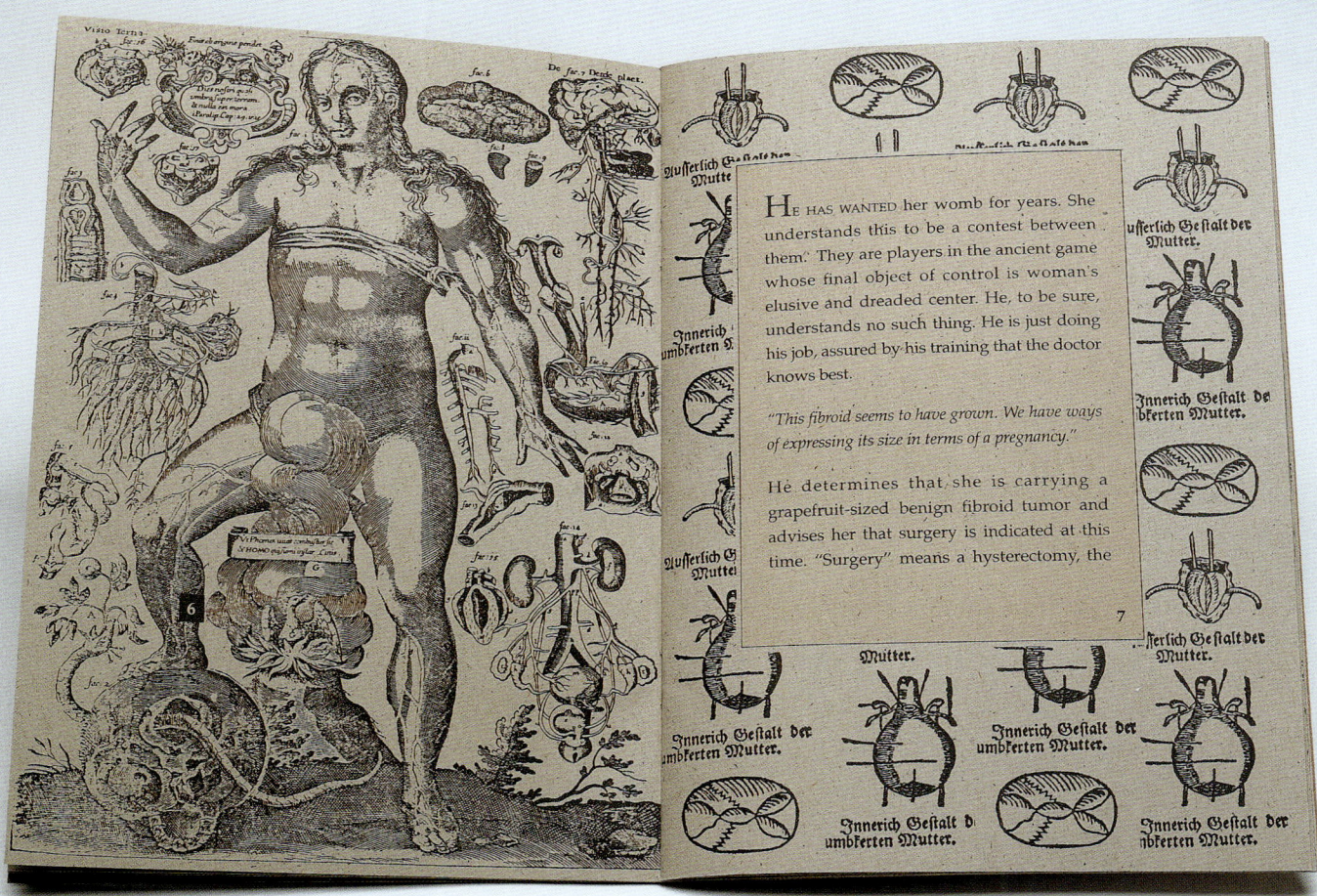

Emily Martin (American, b. 1953)

Eight Slices of Pie, 2002

Inkjet on paper, aluminum and plastic pie pan

10 in. (diameter)

Edition of 25; Naughty Dog Press, Iowa City

Gift of Zena and Arnold Lerman in honor of Iris Greene

When I returned to my studio after the tragedy of 9/11, I abandoned the project I had just begun: a humorous carousel book about nightmares. Reality was nightmarish enough, and it certainly was not funny. During this time I found myself drawing in, thinking about my family, seeking comfort. One day, as I sat with my notebook in a café, I focused on the comforting notion of pie. I began to write, allowing the format of wedge pages to shape the written text. Each slice contains a pie recipe and personal memories and reflections. For example, the recipe for lemon chiffon pie accompanies a story from my past which ends: "The college romance was doomed but my affection for this pie will last forever."

M*y 9 Migraine Cures* records a variety of remedies that my partner Ann Kalmbach has tried to alleviate the excruciating pain of migraines, including massage techniques, hyperventilating, a wrapped head, and aspirin. In the end, only a drug-induced sleep relieves the pain. Each attempt at a cure is depicted with the mantra "not better yet." Ann and I collaborate as KAKE, and this is a KAKE Action Book with a moveable part on every page.

Tatana Kellner (American, b. Czechoslovakia 1950)

Ann Kalmbach (American, b. 1950)

My 9 Migraine Cures, 1987

Offset with die-cuts

9.5 x 13.5 in.

Edition of 300; Visual Studies Workshop, Rochester, New York

Gift of the artists

Lois Morrison (American, b. 1934)

After Water Aerobics, 2002

Plywood, davey board, sand paper, acrylic, Tyvek, paper

18 x 6 x 7.5 in.

Edition of 14; published by the artist, Leonia, New Jersey

Gift of Diane K. Blumberg

As I do my own laps in the pool, I watch water aerobics classes. I have always been amused by the shower caps on heads, tubes between legs, and t-shirts over bathing suits. The people emerge from the pool carrying water noodles, weights, and floats, talking about how good this is for them. I understand: I too feel virtuous.

While devising this book-object, I discovered in an old book a diagram for making a toy, which gave me the mechanism I needed for the raising and lowering of words and figures. Men from a workshop group at Aunt Martha's retirement community in Hackettstown, New Jersey, made the boxes.

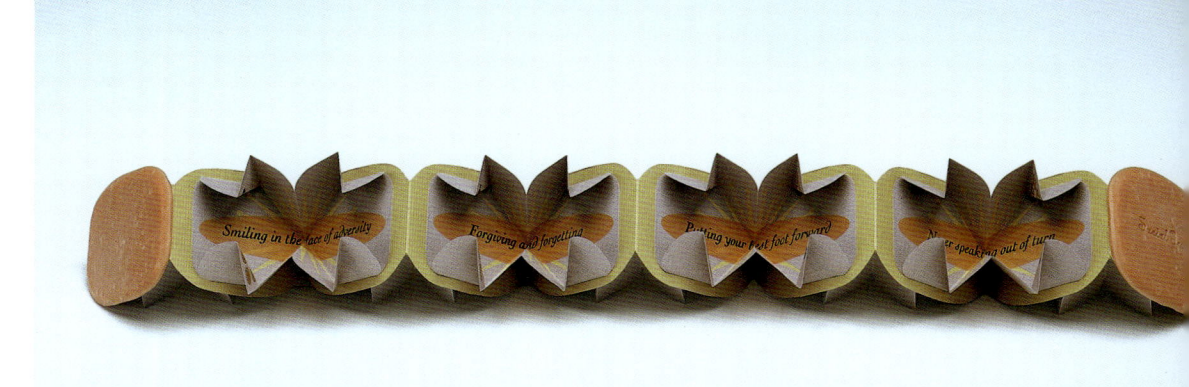

Julie Chen (American, b. 1963)

Bon Bon Mots, 1998

Letterpress on paper, Fimo, polymer clay, Plexiglas

10 x 7 x 2 in.

Edition of 100; Flying Fish Press, Berkeley, California

NMWA Library and Research Center Book Acquisition Fund

I got the idea for the format of *Bon Bon Mots* about two years before I actually made the book. In my mind's eye, I could clearly see a collection of intimate, confectionlike book-objects. They would be so appealing that the reader could not resist holding each one in his or her hand and reading the contents. This, I thought, would be the perfect way to present contents that might not be so pleasant after all. Among the "sweets" in the confection box are a phrasebook of social graces and a calendar recording each day's guilt and worries. The texts mix sadness and sweetness in equal proportions.

Either/Or
Social Graces
Life Cycle
Elegy
Labyrinth
Either
Social Graces

Autobiographers

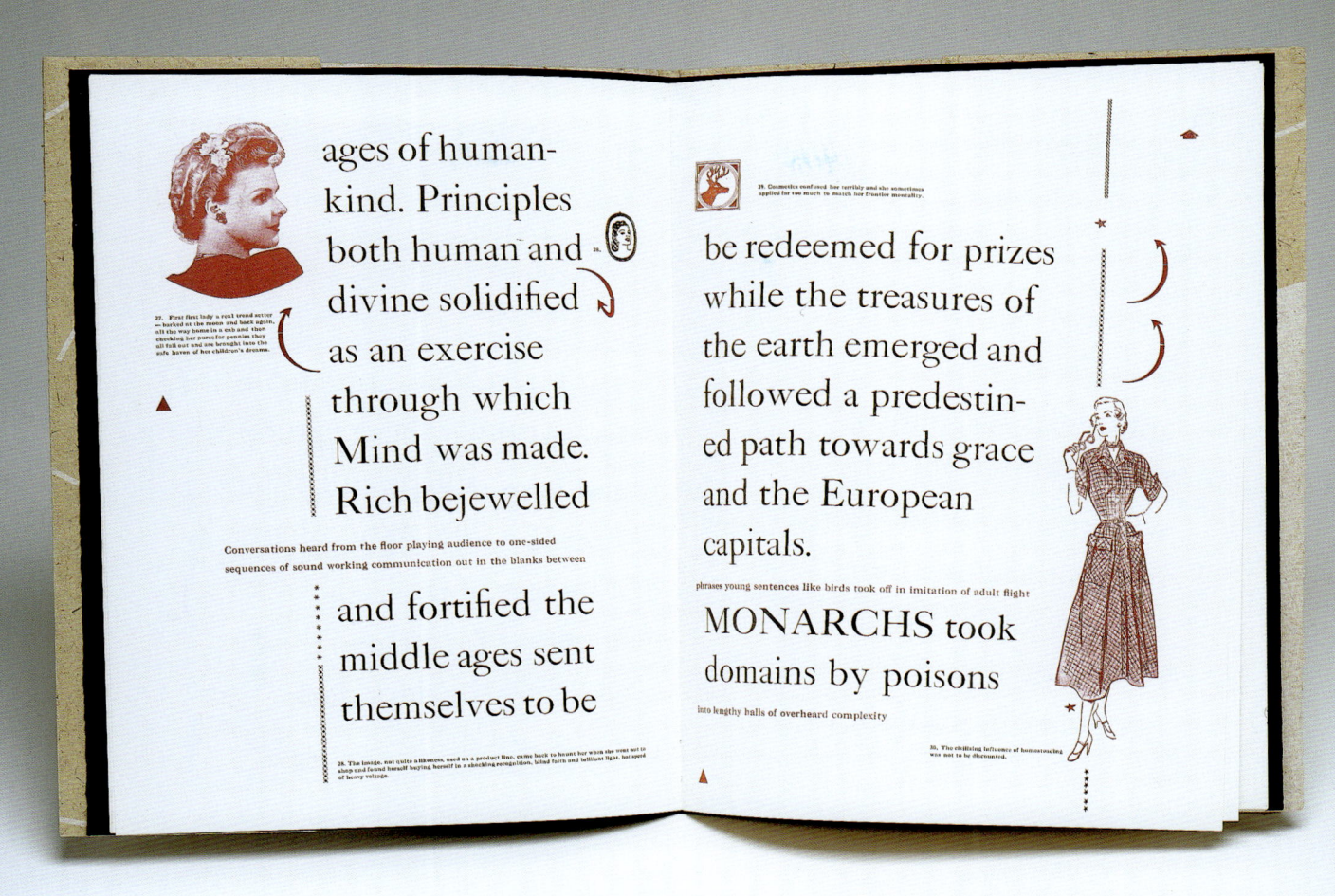

Johanna Drucker (American, b. 1952)

The History of the/my Wor(l)d, 1991

Offset, letterpress

10 x 13 in.

Edition of 70; Druckwerk, New York

Gift of the artist

I came across the image of a drum majorette in Harvard University's collection of paper cuts. My mother, who had died suddenly several years earlier, had been a majorette, and the poignancy of recognition prompted me to produce a work in her memory. It is not maudlin but wry, edgy, and celebratory in the critical vein that had been her manner.

This book is a feminist rewriting of the history of the world and also a critique of feminist orthodoxies about language and patriarchy. I didn't experience language as exclusively patriarchal because it was so bound up in my connection to my mother. In the book, the large black text tells world history, and the smaller red text that breaks through the black recalls my experience of learning language with my mother.

Women and Cars owes a profound debt to Rachel Youdelman's *Water and Power*, an ironic tribute to powerful men and their relationships to water. I remember my first comment after reading it thirty years ago: "Rachel, your next book should be sex and cars, Sex and Cars!" Over the following years, often motionless in the world's longest parking lot known as the Los Angeles freeway system, I realized I should be the one to write that book.

At the time I was intrigued by Hedi Kyle's model for what is now known as the card-structure book. Card pages gave me discrete areas for essays about my mother and aunts' cars. A photo my father took, showing my mother in front of his first car, seemed the perfect image for the book—until I enlarged it to discover that he had focused on the car, leaving my mother's face a blur.

Susan King (American, b. 1947)

Women and Cars, 1983

Offset on paper

5.13 x 6.13 in.

Edition of 500; Women's Studio Workshop, Rosendale, New York, and

Paradise Press, Los Angeles

Gift of Trudi Jacobson

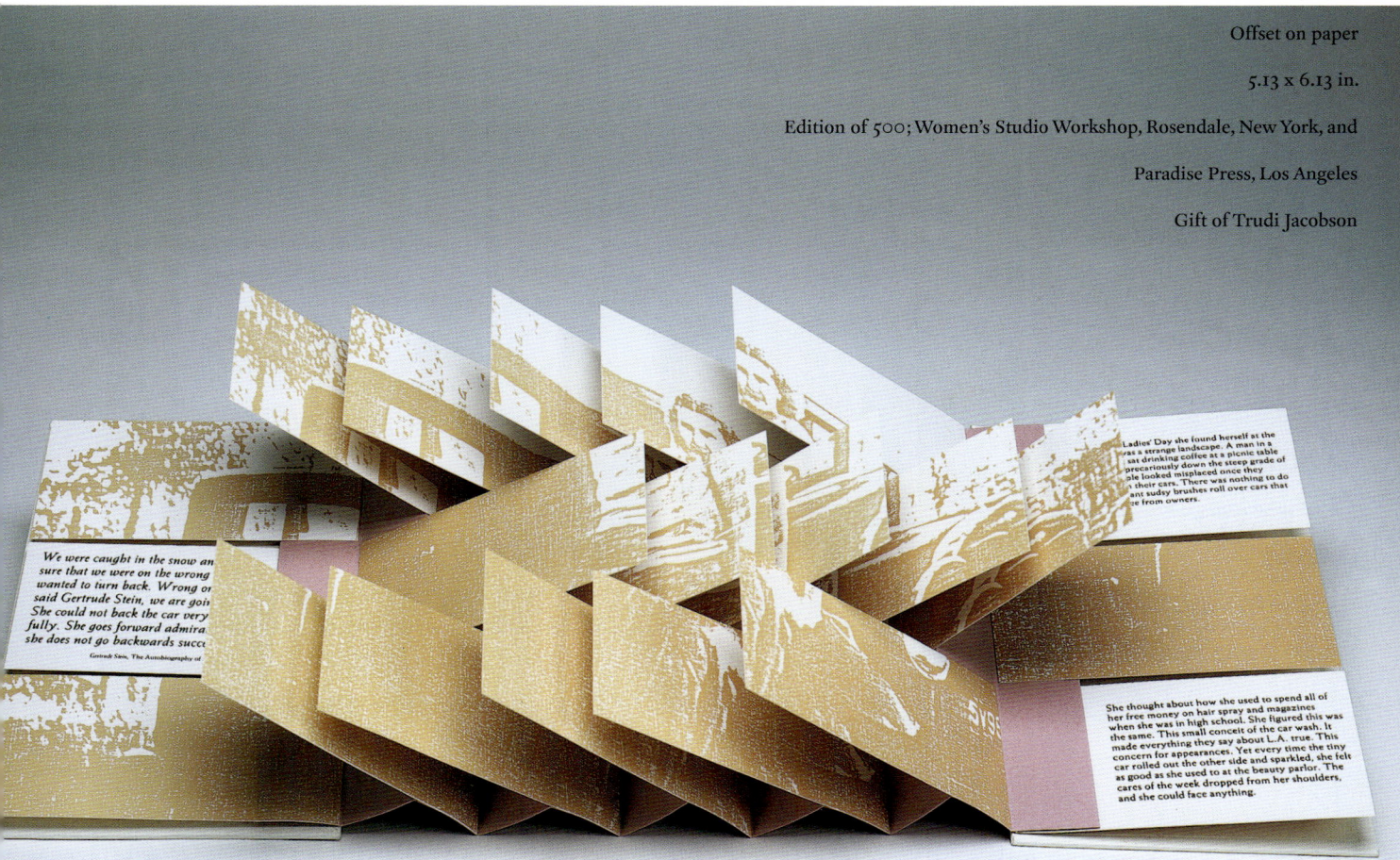

Susan King (American, b. 1947)

Treading the Maze, an Artist's Book of Daze, 1993

Offset on paper and binding board, spiral binding, vellum, acetate

8.25 x 7.5 in.

Edition of 800; Visual Studies Workshop Press, Rochester, New York

Gift of Bernice Baer

Treading the Maze weds two journeys: a sabbatical I took through Europe and Ireland looking at medieval art, and an enforced leave of absence a few months after my return, to recover from breast cancer. Spending time in the land of illness was like traveling through a foreign country. Consequently, what started as an artist's book about travel took on a more layered meaning as I struggled through cancer.

As I labored at my drawing table to refine the structure, I looked up and saw a labyrinth on a poster I'd brought back from France. I found the key to the book: the reader would explore a maze, treading her way through a series of looming images to the center of the book and then reading her way out again. Once inside, she would suffer the disorientation of being lost in a maze, because the book embodies my experience struggling through the labyrinth of illness.

Carol Todaro (American, b. 1956)

i, 2002

Archival ink jet prints on paper

15 x 10 in.

Edition of 10; published by the artist, Miami, Florida

Gift of Nelleke Langhout Nix

In 2002 I was asked to participate in an exhibition called *The Miami Alphabet*, organized by the Miami-Dade Public Library. Fifty-two artists from the region were invited to interpret upper- and lowercase letters of the Roman alphabet.

Charged with inventing a visual representation of the letter "i" and in Paris for an extended stay, I found my "i" in the July Column at the Place de la Bastille. It was the spring of 2002, and all of France was in turmoil over the second-place finish of the right-wing candidate Jean-Marie Le Pen in the presidential primaries. Daily protests at the Bastille were especially impassioned, including the one-man protest I photographed for the book.

I thought it was interesting that a French speaker would choose an expletive in English to register his outrage; while designing the book I began to write a list poem, a glossary of words beginning in "i" in French, whose meaning in English had a freely associated relationship to the situation at hand.

Pamela Spitzmueller (American, b. 1950)

British Museum Memoir, 1997

Pencil on graph paper, copper sheet, copper wire

6.5 x 4.5 in.

Unique artist's book

Gift of United States Department of Education

British Museum Memoir was conceived after my first visit to the British Museum, which at the time also housed the British Library. Numerous exhibit cases displayed books from all over the world and many different time periods. I stayed for hours, soaking in the familiar and the new and strange. Some books were of such unusual shapes and materials that I wrote a text about the experience and decided to try a new material and structure for the book and binding. The content, both images and text, express my reaction to the British Library—I found it frustrating that the books were encased and their contents held secret. It is a bit ironic that this book now lives in a museum as well.

Ghada Jamal (Lebanese, b. 1955)

Back Ground, 1995

Watercolor, acrylic, graphite, collage on paper

Copper cover by Dean Alexander Smith

9.75 x 9.75 in.

Unique artist's book

Gift of the artist

Each page of *Back Ground* is a return visit to my native land, Lebanon, set in the time before violence put an abrupt halt to all of my youthful expectations. The landscape, arabesque design, patina, and patterns are layered to unfold a sense of serenity, peace, and continuity. *Back Ground* grieves the loss of innocence, mourns a dashed dream, and desperately yearns for the beautiful, the mystical, the permanent.

To make the book, I started with slides of landscapes I painted while living in Lebanon. After enlarging and reducing photocopies of the slides, I incorporated the copies into collages with different textures. An arabesque design was used as background for miniature paintings. I commissioned sculptor Dean Alexander Smith to create the metal book cover, which continues the arabesque design.

Katherine Glover (American, b. 1947)

Green Salad, 2001

Vellum, acrylic on Tyvek, semiprecious beads, ribbon, wooden bowl

6.75 x 9.5 in.; bowl diameter 12.5 in. (flat)

Unique artist's book

NMWA Library and Research Center Book Acquisition Fund

Green Salad is a love story. It recalls a day when my sixteen-year-old son and I finished a salad that my lover had prepared the night before, but which he and I had left uneaten. My son found the salad particularly delicious, although the ingredients were quite ordinary, and I mused on the notion that something of my beloved had passed from his hands into the ingredients, conferring a special tastiness. While eating the salad, I was exquisitely engulfed by love for my man and maternal love for my son.

Green Salad's triple Turkish map-fold structure both conceals and reveals a poem nestled in the lettuce leaves, just as love can both hide and manifest itself in such simple activities as preparing and eating food. The principal material, Tyvek, is a spun olefin that can withstand the repeated folding inherent in the book's structure. It also possesses a crisp, rustling quality that strikes me as distinctly saladlike.

In the lab, fragile substances are kept in amber-colored glass to protect them from degradation from light exposure. Similarly, secrets exposed to light lose their power. My secrets are the people I choose as imaginary viewers or recipients of my art. As I work, I feel as if I am in conversation with them, though they are not in the room. These most necessary muses are people in my life or writers known to me only through their words. For this work, I created a flowing, chronological collage of the inspiring women and men in my life. On the back of the scroll are quotations from writers like Eva Hesse, Yukio Mishima, Anais Nin, Robert Penn Warren, Czeslaw Milosz, and three poems that I composed for the book.

M. Jordan Tierney (American, b. 1963)
"She keeps her secrets in an amber jar so the light won't fade them," 2003

Scroll: collage, gouache, acrylic, spray paint, graphite on paper; jar: glass, wood

Scroll: 294 x 5 in.; jar: 11 x 4 x 4 in.

Unique artist's book

Gift of June Rosner

Laura Davidson (American, b. 1957)

Art History Lessons, 2005

Wood, wax, metal, lantern slides, postcards, travel guide pages

4.5 x 5 in.

Unique artist's book

Gift of Lynn M. Johnston

Art History Lessons is about going through the stages of an experience that turned my life upside down: a year of treatment for breast cancer. It was made at a time when I was trying to move from a place of fragility to one of strength and confidence.

The two lantern slides in the center of the book show frescoes from the Arena Chapel in Padua, Italy, painted by Giotto di Bondone in a cycle about virtues and vices. I used his titles: anger and hope. The first and last pages hold vintage postcards depicting sculptures of women. I called the first *melancholy*—she is fragmented, but still stands tall. The last page is *peace*—a woman at peace with herself.

Dreamers and Magicians

Claire Van Vliet (American, b. Canada 1933)
The Dream of the Dirty Woman, 1980

Play by Elka Schumann

Masonite relief prints, collagraph on pulp-painted paper

12.5 x 12 in.

Edition of 85; Janus Press, Newark, Vermont

Gift of Paul Quin, Steven Unger, and Bernice Baer

The Dream of the Dirty Woman is based on a play by Elka Schumann performed by the Bread and Puppet Theater in Glover, Vermont, in 1975 and 1976. The play is set during the French Revolution of 1789 and was inspired by a dream about a woman imprisoned in the Bastille. She is befriended by a female guard who helps her to escape. On the last page of the book we see that the "dirty woman" is dirty no longer. Wearing a beautiful dress and a flower wreath atop her head, the former prisoner is now married to a rich man. The story is told in English by the captive and in French by her Bastille guard. A recording of the play is included with the book. The paper was made with Kathryn Clark at Twinrocker, Brookston, Indiana.

Genie Shenk (American, b. 1937)

Dreamlog, 1995, 1996

Japanese mulberry paper, found paper, acrylic, gouache, ink

2 x 2 x 12 in.

Unique artist's book

Gift of the artist

I trace my interest in dreams to early childhood; I experienced dramatic nightmares and vivid symbolic dreams, many of which I still remember. As an adult, I began to keep dream journals. Jungian philosophy has been a strong influence in my work, and I view the concept of the collective unconscious as a validation for introducing dream material into my art, with the hope that it will evoke in viewers first curiosity, followed by a sense of recognition.

Dreamlog, 1995 is part of a series of daily dream documentations compiled annually since 1982. The pages are two inches square and the book is sixty-one feet long. The titles of dreams are inscribed by hand, and the circles and squares create a repeating mandala pattern. I feel that the spontaneous marks come from the same deep source as the dreams themselves.

Maddy Rosenberg (American, b. 1956)

Shadow of Descent, 2003

Text by H. P. Lovecraft

Digital print, paper

5.75 x 5.75 in.

Edition of 40; published by the artist, Brooklyn, New York

Gift of Lynn M. Johnston

*S*hadow of Descent is my latest collaboration with Hubert Sommerauer. It contains text from H. P. Lovecraft's story "Pickman's Model," the tale of an artist who dares to paint a world beyond this realm. The book pops up into a three-dimensional, fantastical world with shifts in space and time. Cool, strange figures and landscape play off dark architectural mysteries, and both create the illusion of a descent into a lower plane. The entire structure easily folds flat into a square book that nestles in its own box.

In 1970 I lived in Chicago, quite close to the center of the city. Vintage book, antique, and thrift stores abounded in my neighborhood, virtual gold mines for me as I collected all manner of objects and ephemera. I had already begun a series of works based on Poyet and the magical experiments of Tom Tit, and I was ready for an adventure into "real" magic. One day I wandered into the shop of Ed Miller, a retired magician who built and repaired props for other magicians. Mr. Miller became my friend and confidant. He revealed stage secrets and described special effects, and I became determined to find a way to utilize his enthusiastic memories. The solution was the catalogue *Thayer's Quality Magic*. It contained hundreds of illustrated stunts to order, and so I began a series inspired by the descriptions of such amazing productions as "The Phantom Fishbowl," "The Deceptive Change Bag," and "The Bewitched Teacup." These images soon became part of the twelve-page *Wonder Production*, Volume I.

Ellen Lanyon (American, b. 1926)

Wonder Production, Volume I, 1971

Hand-colored lithographs and drawings; paper, graphite, color pencil;

linen and leather binding

20.5 x 15.5 in.

Edition of 12; Landfall Press, Chicago

Artist's proof, gift of the artist

Historians

Sande Wascher-James (American, b. 1946)

How Long? 1994

Liberty Lawn fabrics, color copies, metallic thread, text printed with Gocco

5 x 9.5 in.

Edition of 125; published by the artist, Clinton, Washington

Gift of the artist

In my work I create what I feel will be beautiful and will bring pleasure, which does not preclude having a strong message. Most of my work, which deals with issues of importance to women, is done with what might be considered "women's work": embroidery, quilting, beading, and so on. I do this intentionally to show that there is merit and power in these techniques.

The inspiration for this book came from an article on women's suffrage in *Smithsonian* magazine. I chose quilt blocks to build the image and selected stamps of well-known American women. Purple and gold, the defining colors here, were theme colors of the suffrage movement.

Frances Butler (American, b. 1940)

Confracti mundi rudera (Fragments of a shattered world), 1975

Text by Alastair Johnston and Frances Butler

Handset type on Japanese paper, silkscreened cloth cover

14 x 18 in.

Edition of 60; Poltroon Press, Berkeley, California

Gift of the artist

Confracti mundi rudera was the first of several books in which the images and the text established different streams of speculation, interacting but not necessarily illustrating each other. I combined writings from my own and my press partner's notebooks with drawn images that I based on the thousands of photographs I've taken of everything from roof gutters to clothing to signs to goods in shop windows. An example of the two streams mixing can be seen in the opening sequence: the sea and a dark swan announce the arrival of Beserk, the Viking leader, first off the boat; the second spread describes the continuance of conquest and pillage with swimmers delivering a Colonial-era Indian bed from a late twentieth-century antique shop in Berkeley, California.

Ruth Laxson (American, b. 1924)

Wheeling, 1992

Offset, letterpress, silkscreen on paper

8.5 x 9.75 in.

Edition of 200; Press 63 Plus, Atlanta

Gift of Krystyna Wasserman

Wheeling tackles the car culture in which we live. Its introduction and preface are humorous overviews of the scene. Chapter one deals with a history of the automobile in the world, especially in the United States. Some of the text is concrete poetry, which uses type to form visual images, with occasional drawings in the margins or corners. Chapter two consists of a slightly mad dialog between a woman and a man who is a beleaguered victim of war. They talk about death, God, money, and cars, and the man's automobile almost becomes a third character in the story. The third chapter identifies the two main issues critical to our survival: energy and population. The first is draining away and the second is turning into a flood.

The *Bookano* series of children's storybooks, published in Britain between 1929 and 1949, were among the first pop-up books to be published and were immensely popular. A 1934 edition had an amazing floral pop-up—so beautiful I wanted to imitate it, but not just to make another pretty flower. I wanted to create something bizarrely beautiful, with a closer look revealing a dark surprise that changes the perception of the work. Children in peril the world over had been on my mind, so I made them the subject. The pop-up flowers reveal the tragedy of children in the favelas of Brazil, child soldiers in ravaged Uganda, victims of infanticide in China, and victims of violence and drug addiction in the United States.

Lois Morrison (American, b. 1934)

Endangered Species, 1999

Cloth over board, color-copied drawings, Gocco prints, paper, color pen

7 x 9 in.

Edition of 25; Published by the artist, Leonia, New Jersey

Gift of Lois Pollard Price

Clarissa Sligh (American, b. 1939)

Reading Dick and Jane with Me, 1989

Offset, letterpress

7 x 8.38 in.

Edition of 1,000

Visual Studies Workshop, Rochester, New York

Gift of Clayre Baessler Liammari

The *Dick and Jane* readers from which I was taught in elementary school convinced me that Dick and Jane's white, upper-middle-class suburban family was the norm, and that my family life was an aberration. I created *Reading Dick and Jane with Me* as a site of resistance from which to challenge the message of the old textbooks. In my book, children from my old neighborhood stand in for the characters, and they answer back to authority.

Los dos lados is part of a series inspired by the diary of Anne Frank. I created this book from one of my childhood dresses, with photographs, calligraphy, thread, and the words of this girl forced by the Nazi occupation to take refuge with her family in a small space. Reading the diary affected me profoundly, not only because of its historical impact, but also because it spoke of things I felt—perceptions from the inner world where one is truly alone.

When my mother gave me a few small dresses my sister and I had once worn, it brought me closer to Anne Frank's words of feeling fragile and strong at the same time, knowing that you are growing but have so far to grow, that you are someone but you know not who, that you are just beginning to discover yourself.

Yani Pecanins (Mexican, b. 1957)

Los dos lados (Both sides), 1998

Ink on silk, thread, clothespins, wood

11 x 18.25 x 9 in.

Unique artist's book

NMWA Library and Research Center Book Acquisition Fund

1940–1945
REMEMBERED
translated and retold from my diary

An Artist's Book
BY
NELLEKE NIX

Nelleke Nix (American, b. The Netherlands 1939)

1940–1945 Remembered, 1991

Hand-colored block prints, collage and photo transfers on paper, stamps, fabric, ribbon

7.5 x 10.5 in.

Edition of 125; Nelleke Nix Studio Gallery, Seattle

Gift of the artist

When the Gulf War escalated in February 1991, radio and television aired interviews with civilians, especially those with parents and children in the target zones of Iraqi SCUD missiles. This reawakened many war memories from my early childhood. I decided to write about my experiences in Holland during World War II.

A German ordinance required all people to turn in certain items, including blankets, winter coats, sweaters, bicycles, antiques, and metal objects. Those who complied were given a receipt and were compensated by the Dutch government after the war. My parents and others who had not complied, and from whom the Germans took everything as reprisal, never received compensation because they had no receipt. My father remarked at the time that the Dutch bureaucracy had learned nothing.

After the war, we heard of Hitler's unrealized plan to exchange the Dutch population with that of Poland because he thought the two countries overly nationalistic. We have always been immensely grateful for the Allied efforts to free Europe and end the war.

"And we are here as on a darkling plain
Swept with confused alarms of struggle and flight,
Where ignorant armies clash by night."
—Matthew Arnold, *Dover Beach*

This is an altered book. Static emanates from a radio adhered to the book's cover, as the action unfolds with pop-ups and paper engineered to display the drama of destruction. History has not discouraged war as an answer to conflicting views; even as we adjust to the twenty-first century, we are again at war. *On a Darkling Plain* is part of the war-related art I have been working on in various forms since 1967. There has hardly been a time in my life when our country was not involved in some battle, somewhere.

Sandra Jackman (American, b. 1937)

On a Darkling Plain, 2000

Poem by Matthew Arnold

Altered book, painted and collaged paper, radio, altered toy helicopter,

photographs, bottle, iron stand

17 x 16 x 16 in.

Unique artist's book

Gift of H. G. Spencer in honor of Lorraine Grace

Mirella Bentivoglio (Italian, b. 1922)

The World after September 11, 2001: A Reinforced Book, 2001

Wire, string, paper

10 x 3 in.

Unique artist's book

Gift of the artist

My international background, linked with my inclination toward concrete and visual poetry, directs my creativity to forms of communication in which language is associated with the Esperanto of image. The meaning of *The World after September 11, 2001* is evident in its construction. The wire mesh protects the "fragile" contents: a block of paper labels meant to be torn off and pasted onto shipping crates bound for all parts of the world. The labels are found objects; we are surrounded by potential symbols to be discovered in moments of poetic insight and preserved with the help of forms, words, and materials.

Book in a Cage represents humanity's struggle to communicate, set against the constraints it places on itself that prevent expression. The open door to the cage is a metaphor for the inherent liberty of ideas. The work, which places a French-Italian dictionary behind bars, also touches on the inadequacy of language to express thought and the isolation that can result.

Elisabetta Gut (Italian, b. 1934)

Book in a Cage, 1981

Wood, wire, French-Italian pocket dictionary

5.13 x 4.63 x 4.5 in.

Unique book-object

Gift of the artist

Avian and reptilian brains are simple machines. The decisions they make are immediate: Is this food or poison? Is this a good place for a nest, or will the babies fall to the ground with the next stiff wind? Experience is reduced to binary code: on or off, good or bad, black or white.

Basic principles of biology tell us that humans are distinguishable from their earthly companions by opposable thumbs and the ability to reason—although there are certain primates whose thumbs oppose and certain humans whose reasoning abilities are questionable. My research suggests that remnants of the primitive brain in the human subconscious are activated in periods of high stress, when the imperative course of action is counterintuitive. I would like to suppose that humans can in fact resist the insistent drumming of instinct (fight or flight, fight or flight) and look for the other, the gray, between binary zero and one. In conflict with other human beings, the need to flee or charge may bend to reason, and the reptilian brain may defer to a greater need for peaceful coexistence.

Leah Michelle Geiger (American, b. 1971)

The Reptilian Brain, 2003

Encaustic panels, paper, feathers, quail egg, brass hinges

3.5 x 6 in.

Unique artist's book

Gift of the artist

Mothers, Daughters, and Wives

May Stevens (American, b. 1924)
Ordinary/Extraordinary, 1980

Offset on paper

8.25 x 11 in.

Multiple edition; Lerner Heller Gallery, New York

Ordinary/Extraordinary is a collage of words and images about two important women in my life: my mother Alice Stevens (1895–1986), a housewife and later inmate of hospitals and nursing homes, and Rosa Luxemburg (1871–1919), a Polish-German revolutionary leader and theoretician who was a great inspiration to me. The book includes fragments of Luxemburg's letters sent from prison to her comrade and lover, Leo Jogishes, and excerpts from her political writings illustrated with photographs from her girlhood and her mature years, and with a police shot of her severed head taken after her murder. My mother's words are quoted from letters and postcards and from my own memories. It is important to me that people understand that both words—ordinary and extraordinary—refer to both women.

Mary Perrin (American, b. 1947)

Climbing the Walls, 2003

Altered book, paint, graphite, collage

9 x 16 in.

Unique artist's book

Gift of the artist

Climbing the Walls metaphorically explores the frustrating but seldom talked about experience of being housebound by small children. As a young mother, I was engulfed by the many chores necessary to rear a family. Days and weeks went by with precious little time for such pleasures as making art, and as much as I love my children, this was an extremely difficult situation to endure.

The concept of "nesting" has applications not only in my life but also in my work. It relates to the subject matter and to my methods: just as a bird makes numerous trips to find the choicest bits for its nest, I search for collage materials to interweave and layer on the pages of a book. My family nest is empty of offspring now, but left behind are the twigs, feathers, and scraps that remain on the pages of our book of life.

This work was created as a small, safe, ephemeral space in which to open the door to the first of what seems like an endless stream of fearful discontinuities. From time to time, I become brave enough to open one of these rooms and bathe in its light. For *What's Happening with Momma?* I used my family album and the voice and perspective of a child to critique the construction of family snapshots. The emergence of a memory about my younger sister's birth at home set into motion the making of this piece. At first I saw it as a diptych, but while building and combining text with photographs, I found myself groping for a three-dimensional physical form. The book was made using a Van Dyke Brown alternative photographic process. Negatives were pieced together and contact printed for the house-shaped accordion structure. The interior accordion pieces, printed separately on different paper, were cut, folded, and adhered to the interior of the house structure.

Clarissa Sligh (American, b. 1939)

What's Happening with Momma? 1988

Silkscreen and letterpress on paper

6.5 x 11.5 in.

Edition of 150; Women's Studio Workshop, Rosendale, New York

Gift of Clayre Baessler Liammari

My Mother's Book is made up of the few family stories that have survived my mother's death, along with even fewer pictures. Although this book begins with my grandmother's dream and ends with mine, the voice is that of my mother. I have allowed myself to make such a personal book because the words and images are so typical of my mother's immigrant generation. The structure of the book is a double pamphlet because the variable openings revealing random combinations of texts and images are truer to the structure of memories than a fixed linear progression.

Joan Lyons (American, b. 1937)

My Mother's Book, 1993

Photo offset

6 x 9 in.

Edition of 800; Visual Studies Workshop Press, Rochester, New York

Gift of Krystyna Wasserman

After supper, Alice walked
along the river with her husband
White. She took out her compact
inspected her lipstick
and with a linen handkerchief
blotted the feathery lines
radiating from her mouth.
"You look lovely," White said.
The old rabbit's silky fur
was falling out in patches.
He scratched himself;
dandruff accumulated in the pockets
of his vest. Alice had cropped
her own hair long ago. She smiled,
and smoothed her phantom locks.

A warm breeze caught
the branches of a willow
stirring the surface of the river.
Alice looked into the water
and said, "Do you remember
that episode of *The Twilight Zone*—
the one where the children
dove to the bottom of a swimming pool
and came up in a different world?"
White looked at the sky,
then at his watch. "We'd better go back,"
he said.

Carol Todaro (American, b. 1956)

Looking Glass, 1999

Archival inkjet prints on museum board, venetian-blind binding

1.5 x 15 in.

Edition of 10; published by the artist, Miami, Florida

Gift of Nancy O'Malley

Looking Glass is one of a number of poem-books I've made using my own writing. In this case the poem was inspired by an afternoon walk with my husband in Chartres, France. A beautiful photograph he made there became the background image for the book, in which I imagine Alice and the White Rabbit as a couple, years after their great adventure.

123

Elisabetta Gut (Italian, b. 1934)

Volo-volume (Flight-volume), 1980

Paper, wood, wool, spray paint

15.5 x 15.5 in.

Unique artist's book

NMWA Library and Research Center Book Acquisition Fund

I created *Volo-volume* during a time of personal anguish following the death of my husband. The book opens to the blackest and most disturbing page of my life and marks it with a woolen bookmark. Cotton clouds and seagulls fly away with my happiness. Through the creation of this work, I wanted to express the restlessness of the soul and the immateriality of existence.

I've always known that my parents were Holocaust survivors, though this was never discussed in detail. The only story I remember is one I heard when I was ten years old. My father, while walking with a friend, told the story of being on a ten-day transport from Auschwitz to Brinnlitz without food or water. He recalled hiding behind frozen corpses while other prisoners discussed who their next meal would be. The only other reference my parents made to their suffering was the frequent reminder, "Eat everything; you don't know how lucky you are."

My father lost fifty-three family members in the Holocaust; my mother was the sole survivor from her family. As my parents grew older, it seemed important to record their stories. My parents decided to write their memories in Czech, their native language. While translating, I couldn't visualize the places they were describing. This was in 1990; the Velvet Revolution had just happened, and I was able to travel to Czechoslovakia without fear of being imprisoned. While there, I photographed the sites, and I used the images, along with family photographs, in this book. I chose to have the viewer see my father's arm with its ineradicable number at all times, to ensure that the person who bore the number will be remembered.

Tatana Kellner (American, b. Czechoslovakia 1950)
B-11226: Fifty Years of Silence, 1992

Silkscreen, cast handmade paper

20 x 12 x 3 in.

Edition of 50; Women's Studio Workshop, Rosendale, New York

Gift of Lynn M. Johnston

Working in the book arts has led me to explore different elements of memory. Often when making a book, I hear the silent voices of distant places and times, and I feel myself standing at the intersection of two histories—my past crossing into my future.

The Diary of a Sparrow is what my grandfather, Enji Watanabe, called the journals in which he recorded the events and circumstances of his life. Beautiful brush-strokes fill these journals, which are written in an archaic literary style of Japanese that young people no longer understand. In 1996, nearly thirty years after my grandfather's death, my mother pulled out eight volumes of his journals and told me she hoped someone would translate them.

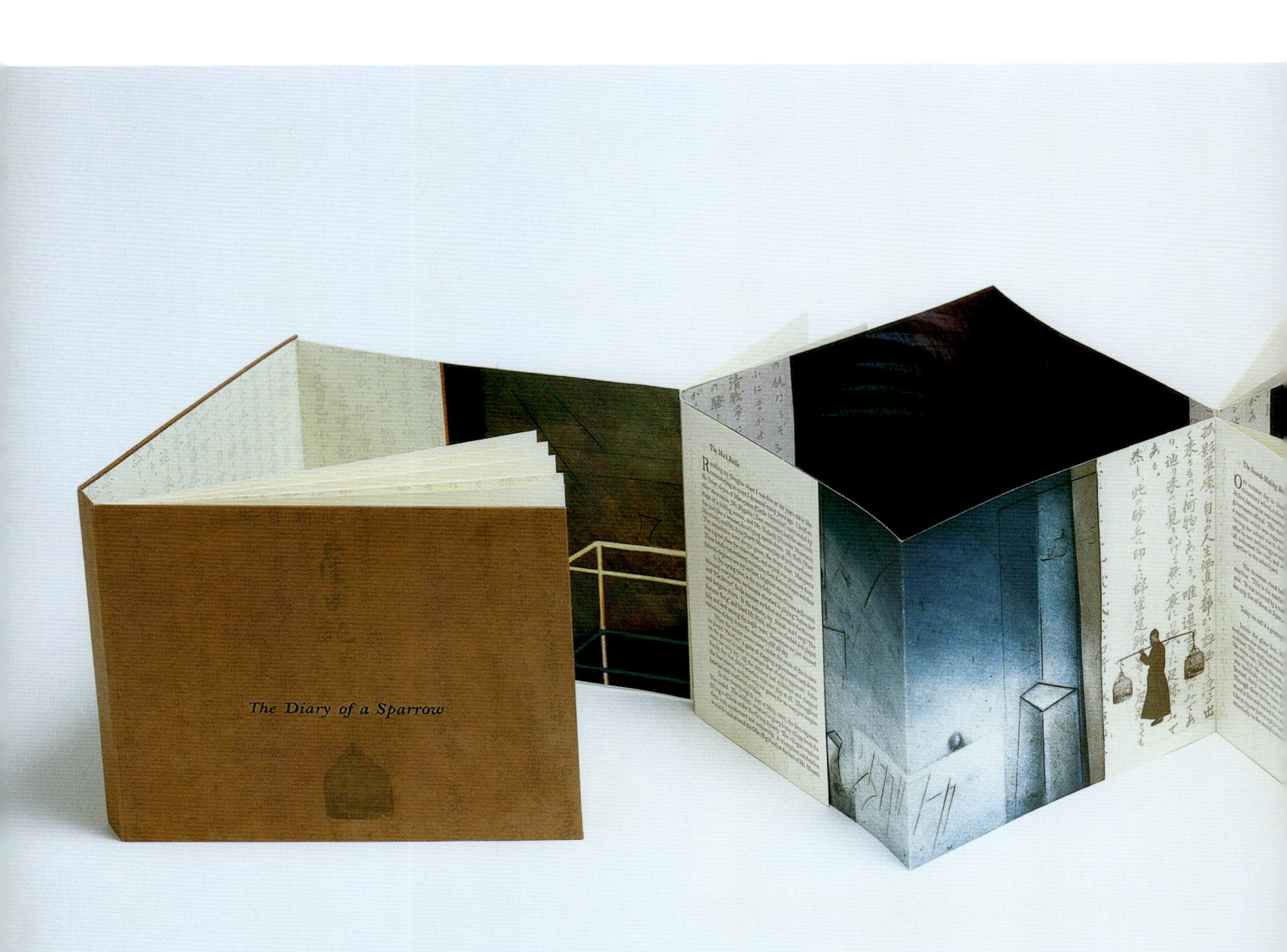

Of course I translated them—into modern Japanese and into English—and I discovered the history of a simple people living within a small stretch of land, their gentle lives tossed by the upheavals of war and the encroachment of the modern world. Wishing to convey the rich and thoughtful journey of *The Diary of a Sparrow* to a wider audience, I designed and made this book of text and images. The binding design enables the book to unfold and stand on a table like a small Japanese house.

Kazuko Watanabe (Japanese, b. 1949)
The Diary of a Sparrow, 1999

Diary by Enji Watanabe

Multiple-plate color etchings, computer-manipulated photoetched images, handprinted on European and Japanese paper

9.25 x 7.5 in.

Edition of 125; published by the artist and NMWA Library Fellows

Gift of NMWA Library Fellows

Travelers

Elsi Vassdal Ellis (American, b. 1952)
The Final Nile Journey, 1993

Pencil on paper, Egyptian papyrus on cover

8.75 x 9 in.

Unique artist's book

Gift of the artist

The Final Nile Journey is a return to the magic time in my life when I believed I would be the next Howard Carter and make my mark in the field of archeology. I read anything I could find in the library or could afford to buy with babysitting money. (I still own the first paperback on Egyptian archeology I ever bought.) Later I was disappointed by a college recruiter who impressed upon me the difference between "man's work" and "woman's work" in archeology, and I made the decision to study visual communication.

This book is the very first I created reviving my teenage archeological fantasies. It has been followed over the years by other Egyptian tales, a Chinese love story with dragons and emperors, a nine-book exploration of Aztec creation stories, and several others.

Carol Barton (American, b. 1954)

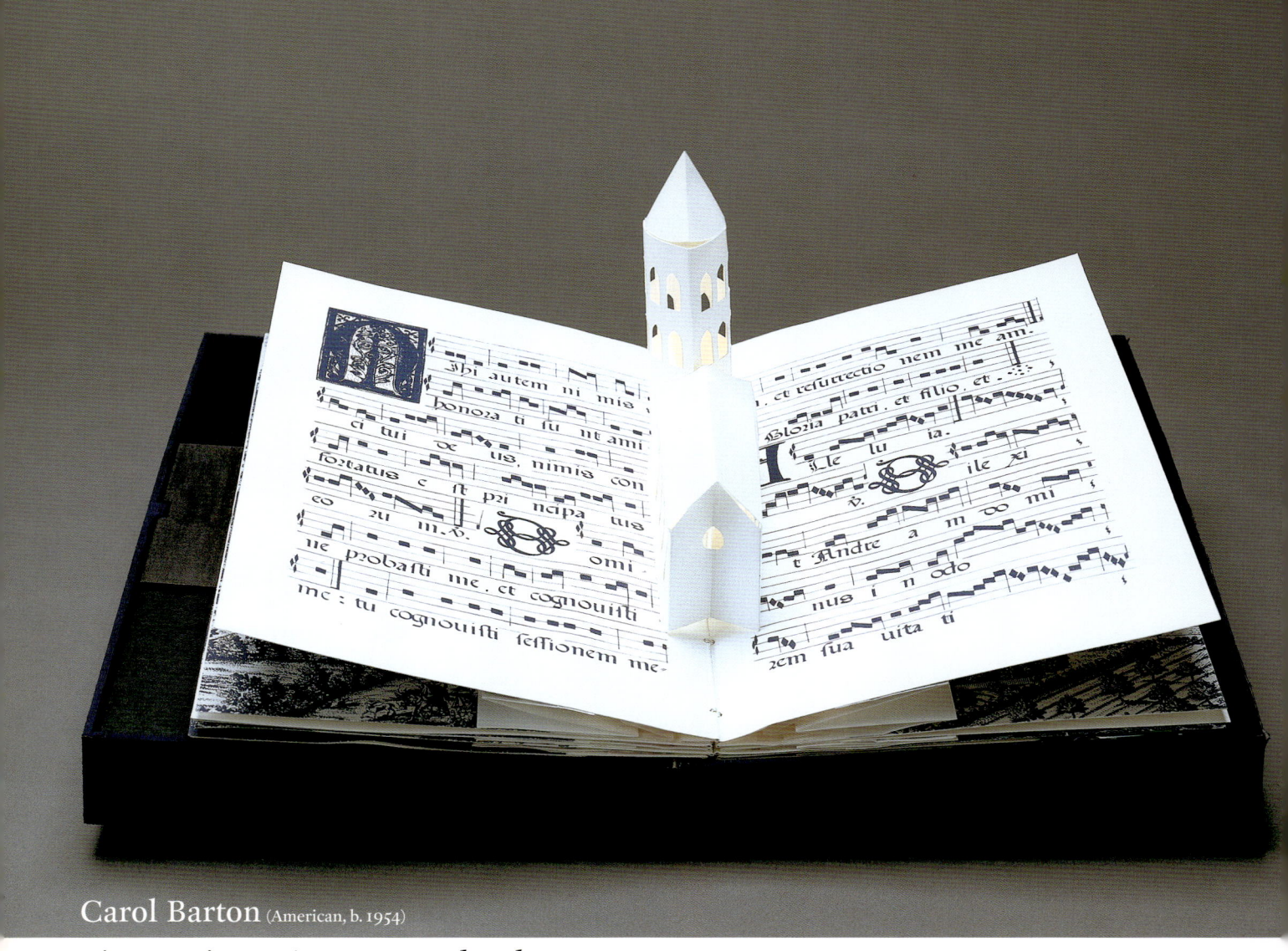

Five Luminous Towers: A Book to be Read in the Dark, 2001

Offset print, bulb, wire, board, Japanese book cloth

7.5 x 11.5 in.

Edition of 50; Popular Kinetics Press, Glen Echo, Maryland

Gift of United States Department of Education

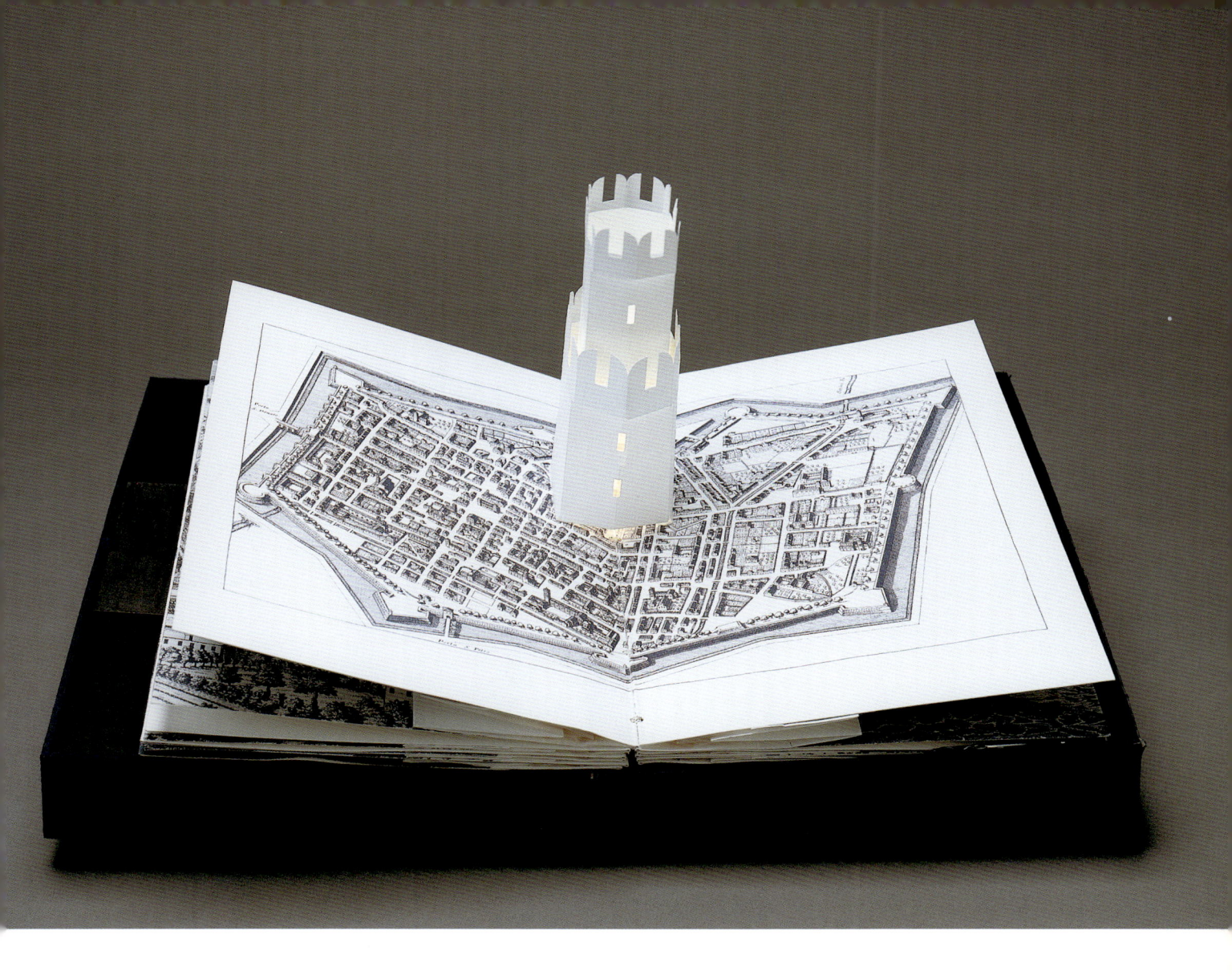

A residency at the Bogliasco villa in Genoa, Italy, brought an unexpected element to my work. I visited many towers during my stay—famous ones such as the leaning tower in Pisa, and obscure ones in small northern Italian towns. I looked at the architectural elements that distinguish the various functions towers have served throughout history, and I researched towers in local libraries. At the same time, I was surrounded by resident poets and scholars at the villa and found inspiration in their writings for my poems. I was amazed to discover how easily the words came.

The idea for a book with an interior light source had come to me years before, but in Italy I was inspired to revisit the challenge of combining light and paper engineering in an artist's book. I envisioned a volume of dimensional towers where light and shadow played against the architecture of pop-up paper structures.

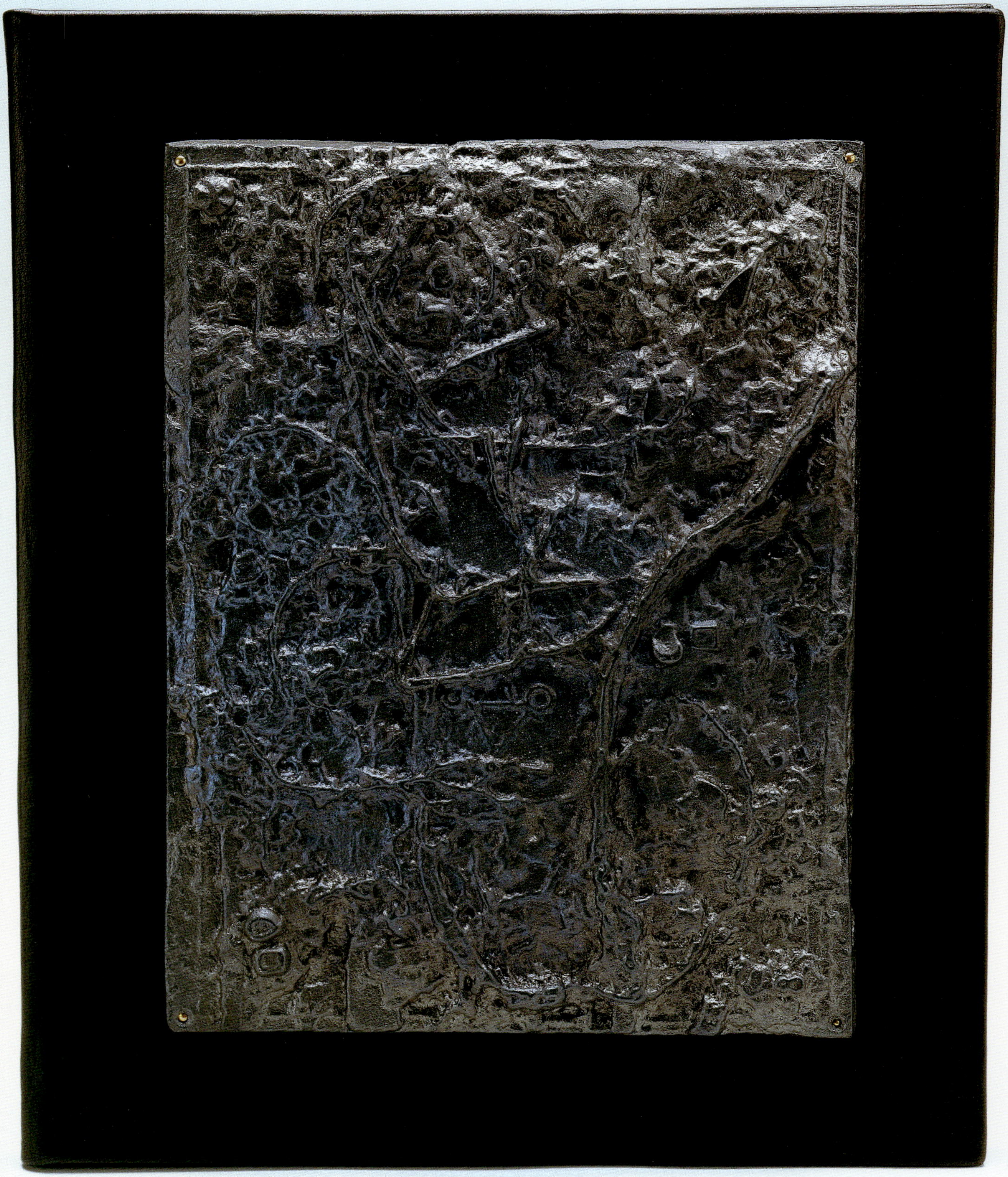

Susan Harlan (American, b. 1950)

Song Lines, 1993

Photo silkscreens, letterpress, engravings on Japanese paper, anodized aluminum, Italian linen cloth on book board

9 x 11 in.

Edition of 125; Published by the artist and NMWA Library Fellows

Gift of NMWA Library Fellows

Song Lines was inspired by a trek through Australia. While there I learned that Aboriginal people retrace the journeys of the Creation Ancestors by singing songs that weave navigational paths through the open plains from one place to another. The cadence and rhythm of the songs mark the steps to each waypoint.

I am fascinated by all kinds of maps because of their practicality and their metaphorical richness. This book is an exploration of my journeys in everyday living and an acknowledgment that my numbered days are flying by and I haven't unraveled the mystery, and I probably never will.

Karen Kunc (American, b. 1952)

On This Land, 1996

Poem by Lenora Castillo

Woodcut on paper and walnut stain on flax paper

5.25 x 7.5 in.

Edition of 125; published by the artist and NMWA Library Fellows

Gift of NMWA Library Fellows

My lifework is thinking on, and looking at, how life is lived the world over—how work is done, how nature is shaped, how human and natural forces impact our lives. These thematic threads become a metaphor for my own creative processes. Images suggestive of landscape, open farms, and contrasting sky visually create a horizontal poetic line in this accordion-fold bookwork. In a simple voice, Lenora Castillo's poem tells of dislocation from Mexico to Nebraska, the strangeness of a new place, and the gradual acceptance of austere beauty. Hand-printed woodcuts and the letterpress-printed poem make a tactile and colorful interpretation of earth and human presence.

This artist's book was inspired by the iconic Australian ballad "Waltzing Matilda," written by A. B. (Banjo) Patterson. The story is of a *swagman* (itinerant worker) who steals a *jumbuck* (sheep) for his dinner. When approached by the police, he boasts, "You'll never catch me alive!" and drowns himself in a *billabong* (waterhole).

The illustrations are original relief etchings. The cover paper is monoprinted, using actual Australian plants as the images. The volume is enclosed in a sewed and stenciled cloth *tucker* (dinner) bag, a reminder of the swag in which swagmen carried their belongings while on the move.

Philippa Webb (Australian, b. 1933)

Waltzing Matilda, 2004

Etching, monoprint, calligraphy, handmade papers, stenciled cloth

12 x 11.5 in.

Edition of 20; published by the artist, New Farm, Australia

Gift of Nelleke Langhout Nix

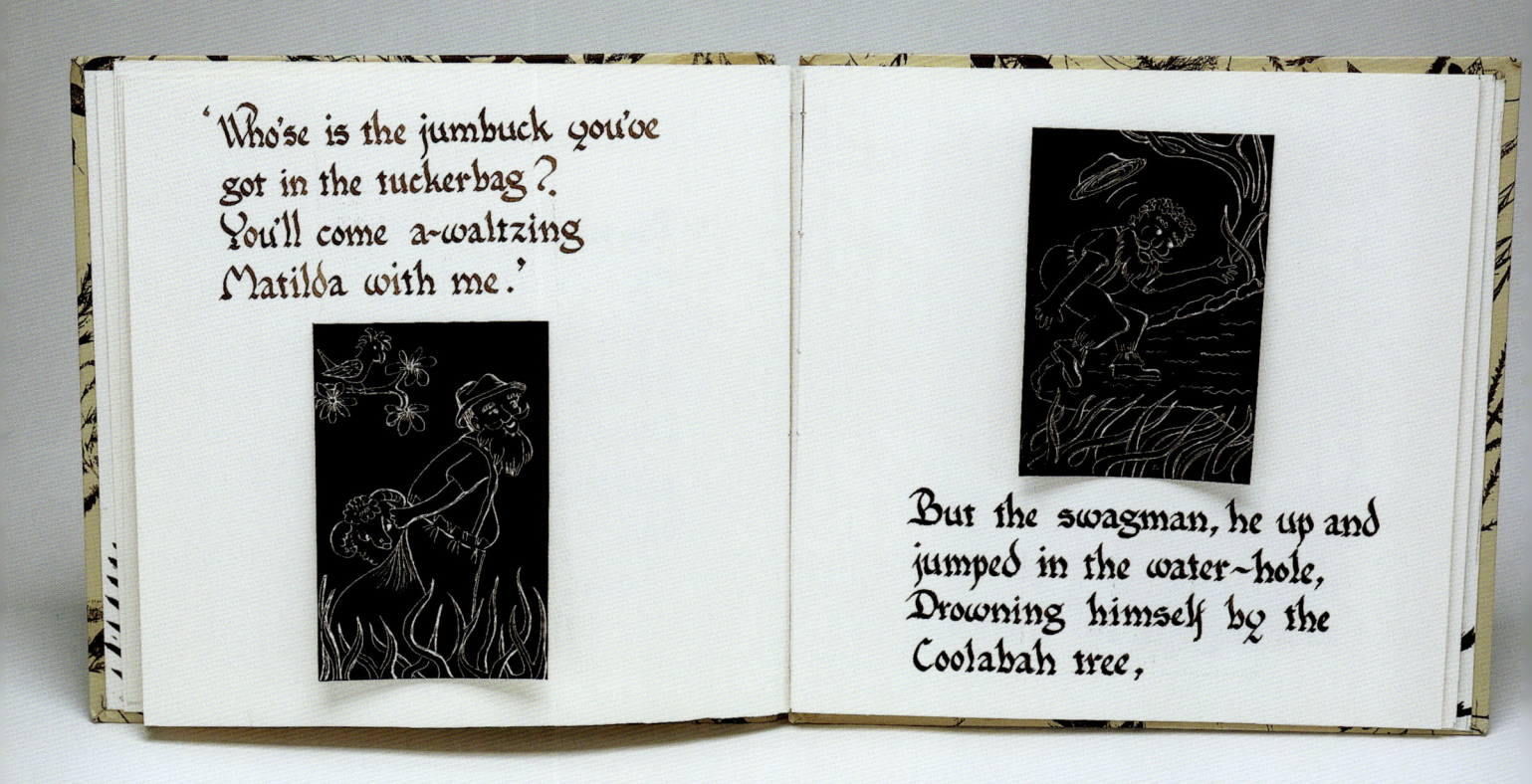

Carol Schwartzott (American, b. 1945)

Kimono/Kosode, 2002

Letterpress on hand-dyed paper, Chiyogami paper, mat board, basswood dowels

6 x 10.5 x 2.5 in.

Edition of 125; published by the artist and NMWA Library Fellows

Gift of NMWA Library Fellows

Kimono/Kosode is a history of the kimono. It was a technically demanding book to make, with die-cuts, laminating, letterpress, and a complex structure meant to evoke the many graceful layers of traditional Japanese dress. The book can lie flat, but when displayed on its edge with the pages open, a tiny multidimensional theater appears and the kimono becomes a window.

Susan Allix (English, b. 1943)

The Beach: A Short Story, 1989

Etching, linocut, woodcut, pen-and-ink drawing, gouache, crayon, leather, cotton, sea shells

10.25 x 8.25 in.

Edition of 18; published by the artist, London, United Kingdom

Gift of Herrick Jackson

The Beach lives in a blue-striped beach bag, a few collected shells threaded on its drawstring. Evoking the breezy, casual, outdoor life of the beach, where landscape, people, and behavior follow certain patterns prompted by the seaside environment, the book was designed from drawings made while observing summertime life on the shore. This scene-setting is a visual guide to the story. The "text" has no words, only punctuation, so readers must supply their own interpretation and mentally write their own drama, thus personalizing the book. The punctuation creates its own life and story—an inverted question mark suggests a Spanish voice, for example. The book was made at a time of discussion about the necessity of words in artists' books. *The Beach* is a comment on this, exploring the ambiguity between visual and verbal responses and creating a suspended situation of infinite possibilities.

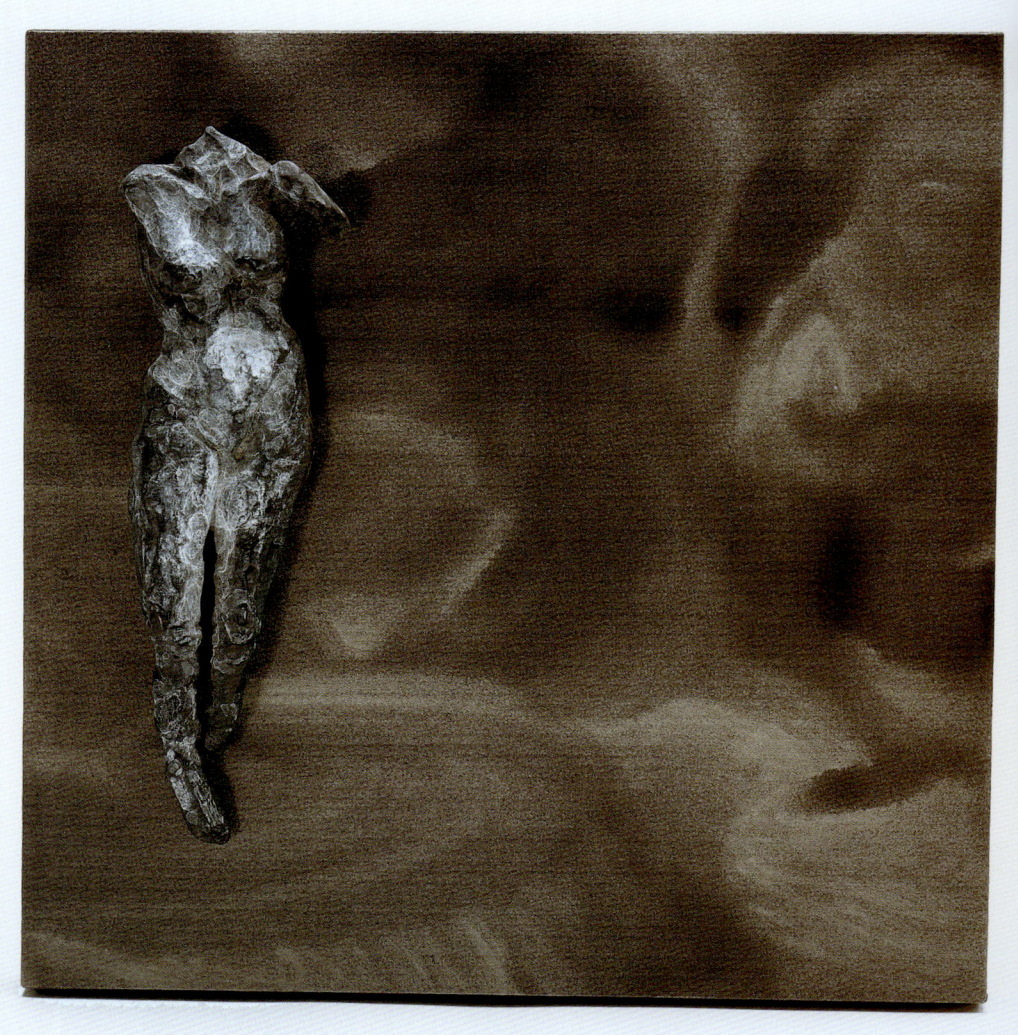

Michele Burgess (American, b. 1960)

Sleeping Inside the Glacier, 1997

Poem by Sandra Alcosser

Book: etching and collagraph on Roma, Lana, and Japanese handmade paper, letterpress; slipcase: vellum, paste paper, cast bronze

7.25 x 9.75 in. (book); 9.75 x 10 in. (slipcase)

Edition of 35; Brighton Press, San Diego

Gift of Kathi George

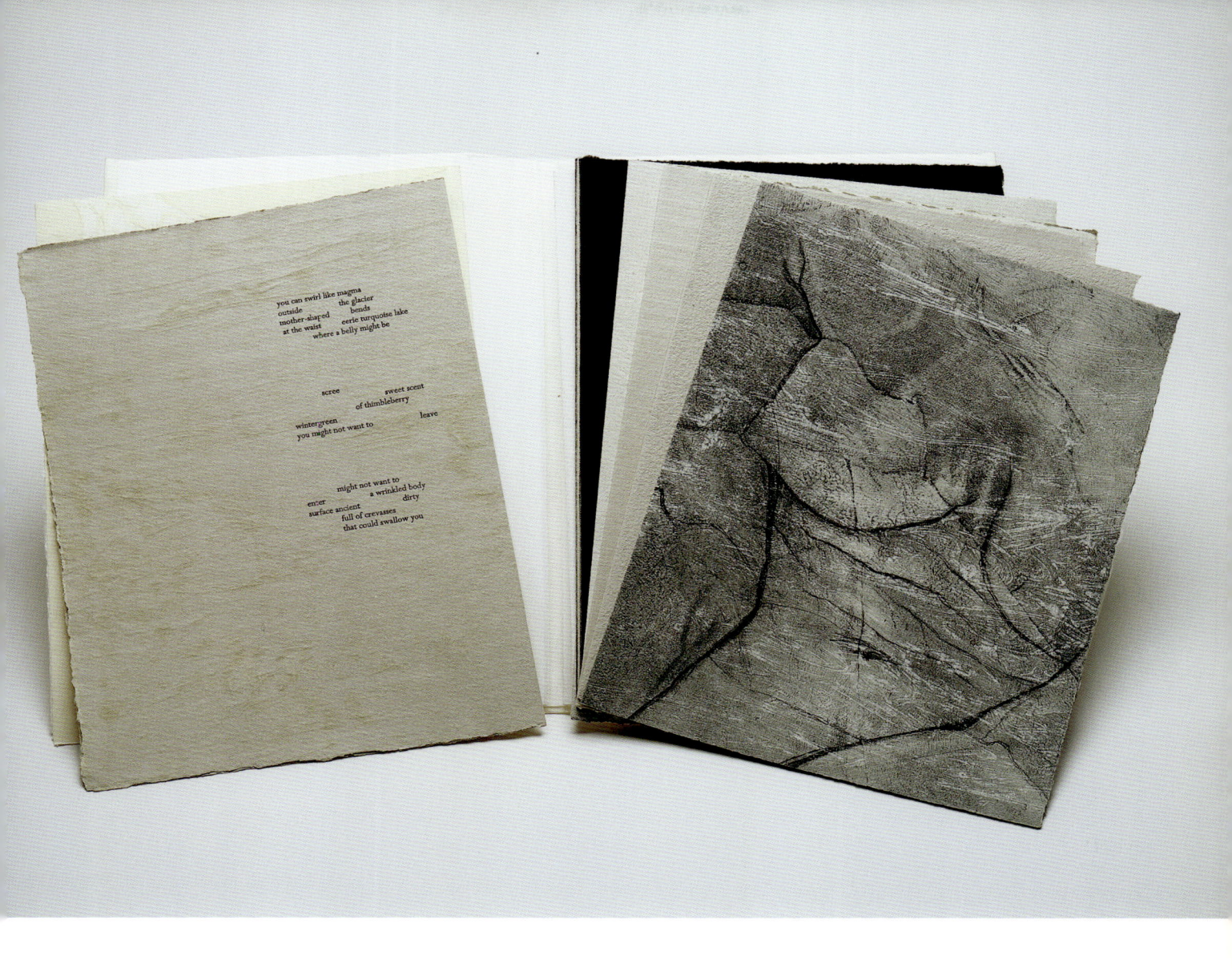

Sandra Alcosser and I have collaborated on four books, after realizing early on that our work had recurring themes dealing with women in the Western landscape. In *Sleeping Inside the Glacier* a woman traveler, frozen in time, is revealed through melting layers of narrative in four voices and the image of lost ships frozen in the glacier. An etching plate, a human body, and a page with text running across it become a landscape in the form of a book that bears the words and the presence of the woman traveler. The last element added to the book was the bronze figure, which assumes the temperature of its immediate environment.

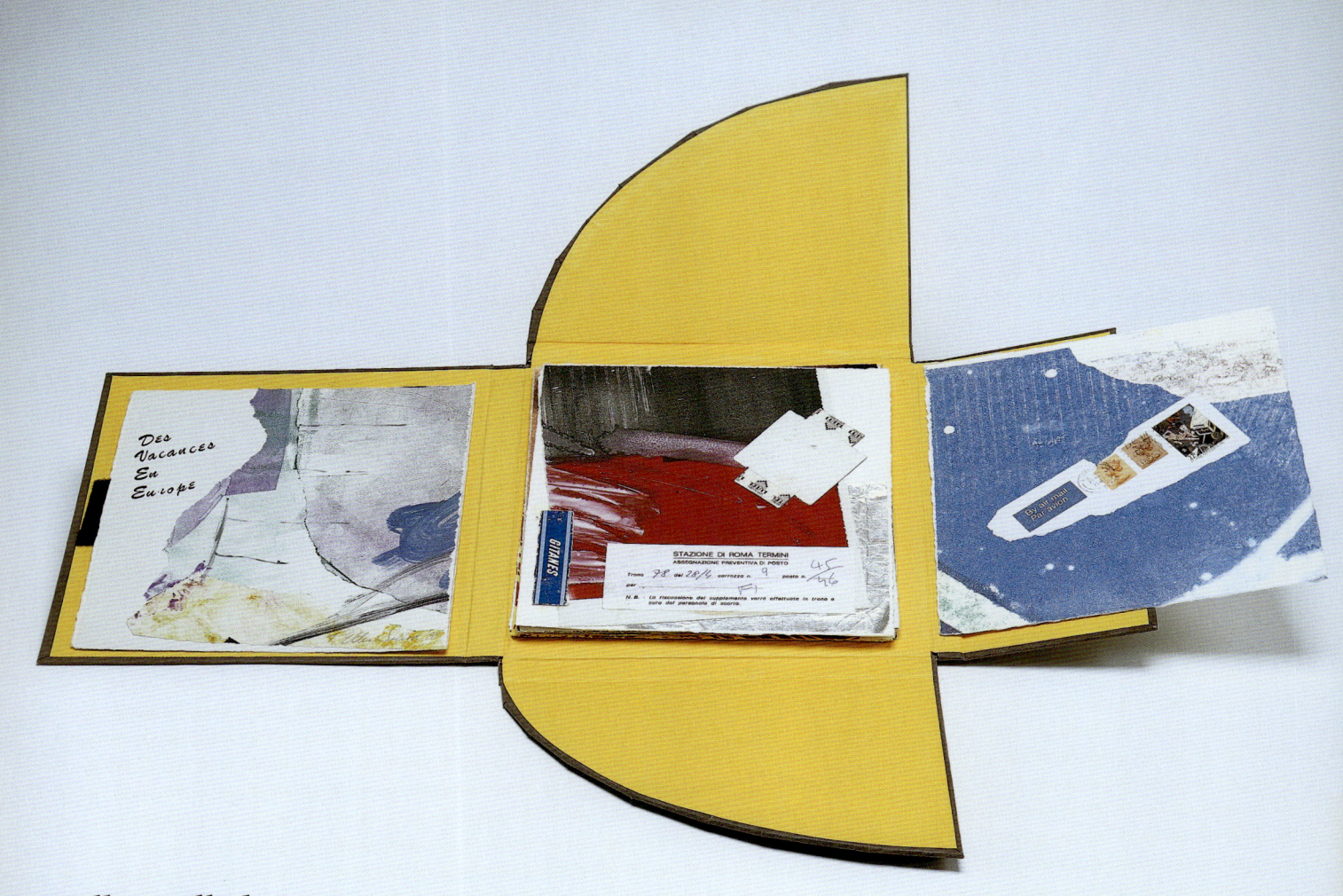

Ellen Sollod (American, b.1951)

Des vacances en Europe (European vacation), 1988

Monotype and collage on paper

8.5 x 8.5 in.

Unique artist's book

Gift of the artist

Des vacances en Europe was created after an extensive trip to Italy and France. Utilizing bits of paper, ticket stubs, and fabrics gathered through my travels, I created a chronology of the experience. The portfolio of loose pages is read sequentially, beginning with the flight across the ocean and ending with the night of my return. In between, the experiences are metaphorically illustrated through monotypes and collages. The loose sheets are collected in a handmade box that opens sequentially to reveal the title page. The book cover incorporates a used entry ticket to a museum, suggesting admittance into the world of travel.

While driving down a major Mexican toll road, I noticed that I never saw dead animals, unlike my home state's US 81, where road kill is ubiquitous. But once in a long while there would be a dead dog on the opposite side of the long fence that ran parallel to the road. From my imagination came the character of the Mexican dog-tosser. This book is an extension of that odd fantasy. When the dog-tosser goes home to bed, perhaps he dreams that dogs follow him. Or maybe he dreams that they bay at him from hell or fly iridescent and winged in heaven.

The limbs of the dog-tosser figure are fastened with grommets to allow him to move and "act" within the book. The reverse side shows dogs growing wings and flying to heaven over a panorama of mountains and plains.

Lois Morrison (American, b. 1934)

The Mexican Dog-Tosser, 1995

Gocco printed on paper with ink and watercolor embellishments

4.25 x 7 in.

Edition of 25; published by the artist, Leonia, New Jersey

Gift of United States Department of Education

In 1988 I returned to Paris after a year of teaching English in Beijing, and I knew I would have to assimilate this profound experience in some way. I grappled with a very strong impression left by the bittersweet nature of Chinese life, in which objects, landscapes, and people could be sublimely beautiful and generous but situations could arise that were harsh, ugly, frustrating, and complicated. I found a text to express this ying/yang feeling, written in 1926 by Lu Xun, China's most famous twentieth-century author. Hoping to see the emergence of a new and modern China from a Great Wall mentality, he writes of the contradictions inherent in this great human construction: its monumentality and the suffering that took place in its building. Going further, he compared it to the mental walls that surround all of us in our approach to changes in our lives. "A curse on this wonderful Great Wall," he cries.

Shirley Sharoff (French, b. United States 1936)

The Great Wall, 1991

Text by Lu Xun

Etching and letterpress on paper

267 x 5.5 in. (open)

Edition of 65; published by the artist, Paris

Gift of Barbara D. Mitchell

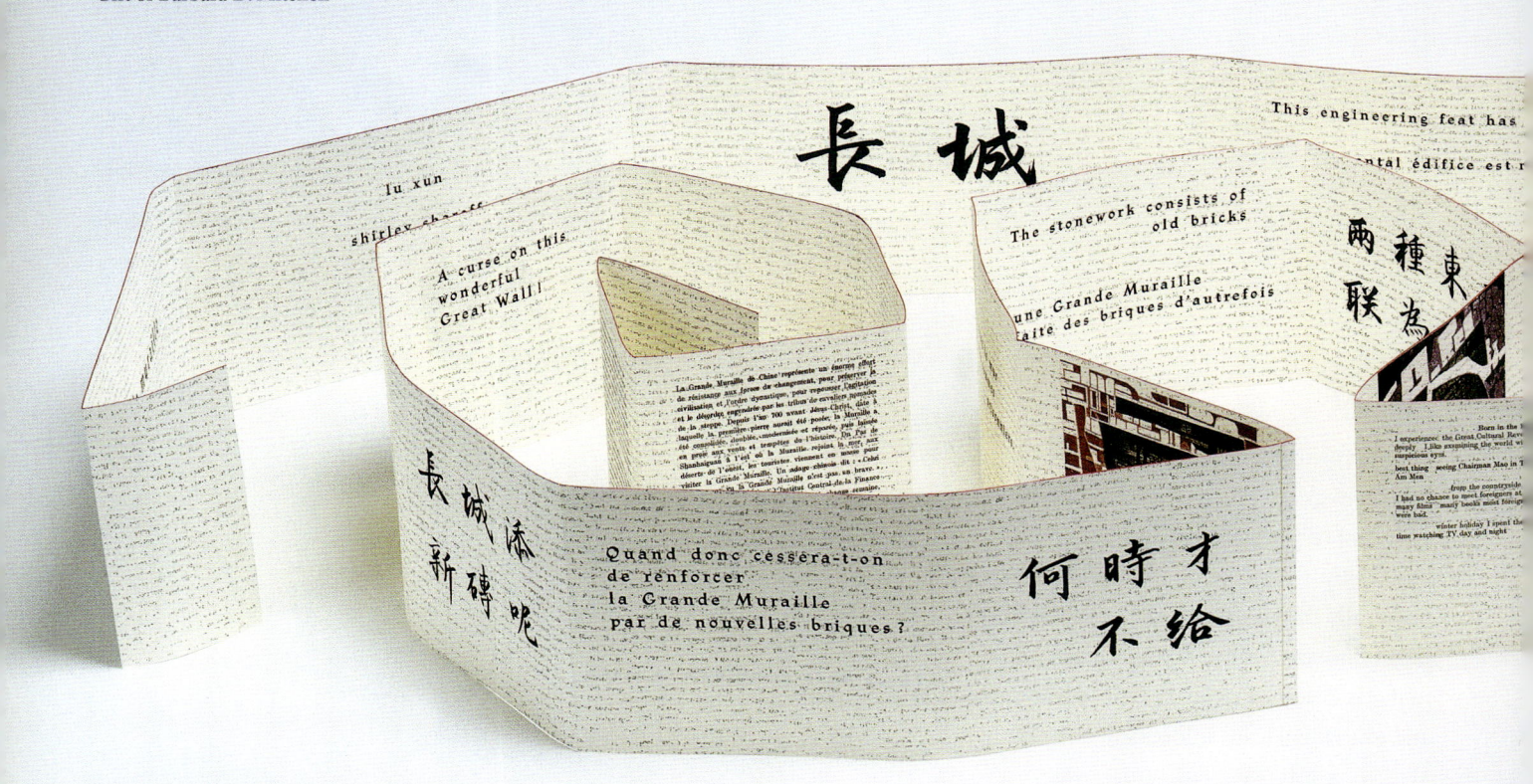

As an English teacher, I assigned my young Chinese students short compositions so they could practice writing, but for me it was a way into their lives and their memories of life in the 1970s. I put extracts from these writings into my book to act as a counterpoint to the solidity of the Great Wall and as an indicator of the impermanence of everything. *The Great Wall* unfolds to a length of seven meters and can be stood up to make a wall of paper. The etchings are of two kinds: the first four allude to Chinese wall hangings and entrances, while the second four point to segments of the Great Wall that are transformed into the walls of buildings and cityscapes. The text is in English, French, and Chinese. The conception and typography are part of a collaboration with François DaRos. Viewed from the top, the book reminds me of the labyrinth found in the Old Summer Palace outside Beijing.

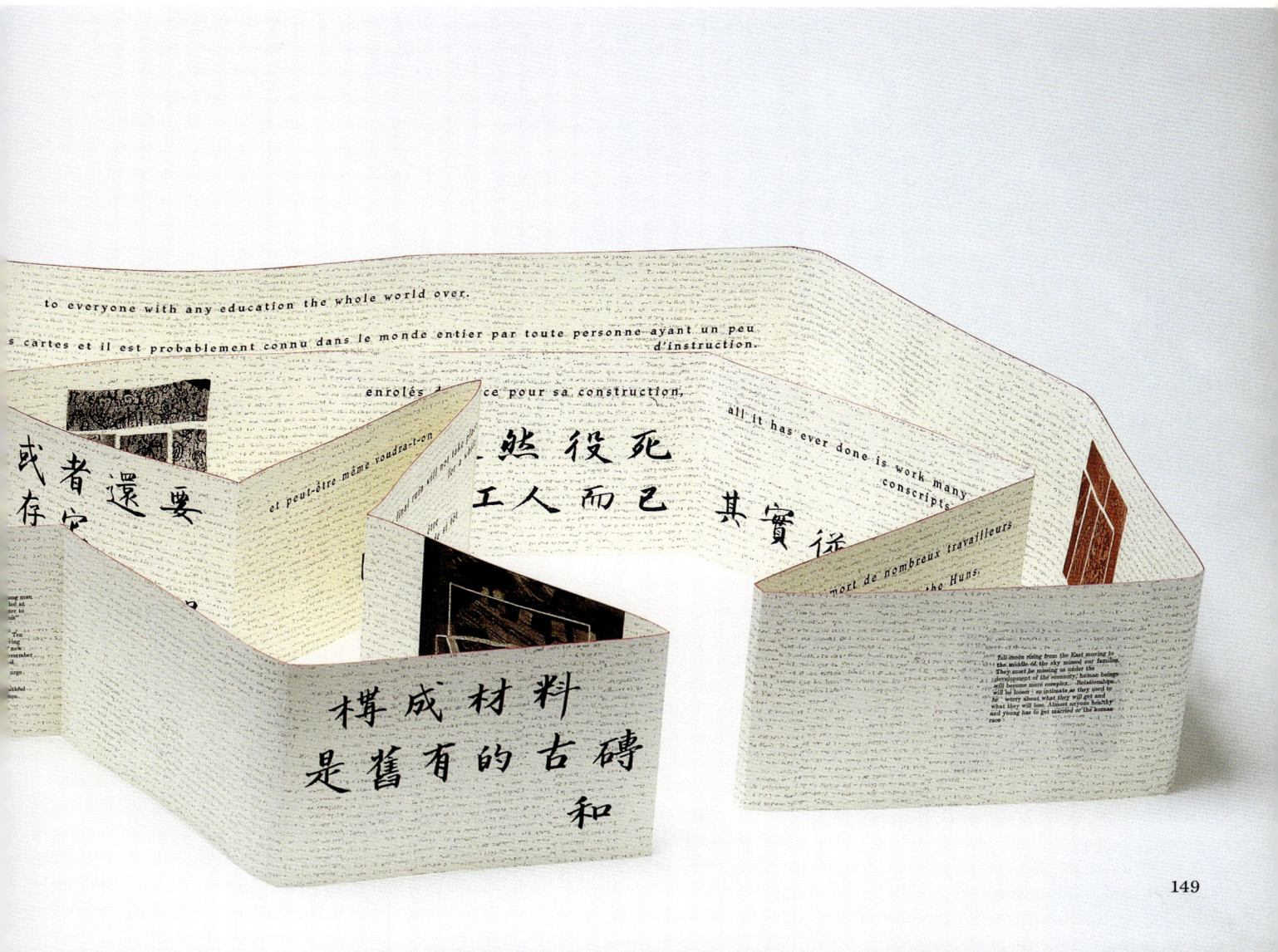

Inspired by the Muses

Mirella Bentivoglio (Italian, b. 1922)
À Malherbe (To Malherbe), 1975

Onyx

7.13 x 5.38 x 2.25 in.

Unique artist's book

Gift of the artist

À Malherbe is dedicated to the French renaissance poet François de Malherbe, whose famous poem "Consolation à M. Du Périer" deals with the death of Du Périer's young daughter. The brevity of her life is compared to that of a rose: "Et rose elle a vécu ce que vivent les roses / L'espace d'un matin" (A rose, she has lived as long as roses live / The space of a morning). My book, realized in rose-colored onyx, extends the allusion to the color of dawn and a life of which the only memory is its early and most beautiful phase.

Mirella Bentivoglio (Italian, b. 1922)

Litolattine, 1998

Iron, tin cans, caps

4.5 x 5.25 x 1.75 in.

Unique artist's book

Gift of Lois Pollard Price

Litolattine is made from tin cans crushed in the street by the wheels of automobiles. It refers to the very first books in art history to be made with unorthodox materials: Futurist books from the 1930s, which were constructed of cigar and sardine tins produced by the Litolatta company. My own book derives from found objects that are charged with signs of former lives and experiences.

Jan Owen (American, b. 1947)

First Brush Stroke, Books 1, 2, and 3, 2001

Poems by John Tagliabue

Acrylic on paste paper

Each panel 14.5 x 14 in.

Unique artist's books

NMWA Members' Art Acquisition Fund

First Brush Stroke began with three long panels of golden yellow paste paper. Just as I was considering what words to write, one of my favorite poets, John Tagliabue, sent me a poem that became the key: "The first brush stroke, now where will we go? . . . Order will be made like still music." All the poems in this piece are by Tagliabue because they sing about words, color, spirit, dance, and love. His *New and Selected Poems: 1942–1977* is one of the most dog-eared books I possess, and I appreciate that he allows me to change his line breaks. With a large brush and a dish of sumi ink, I made a big mark, surveyed it, and began building the columns of words: "Imagine that—let us get together and erect the 1st letter of the alphabet and then the next."

Jan Owen (American, b. 1947)

Hieroglyph, 1999

Acrylic and ink on paste papers

19 x 10.5 in.

Unique artist's book

NMWA Library and Research Center Book Acquisition Fund

Each of my pieces begins with paste paper, a spontaneous and tactile way to create color and pattern. The layers of color contrast with the tight columns of calligraphy. Blocks of woven, painted Tyvek are done last to add texture and to serve as another coded language. When I decided to work on paper on a large scale, I did not want to frame, so I began making hanging accordion-fold books. When making the paste paper for *Hieroglyph,* I scraped away curved shapes in the second layer of color. The form that emerged reminded me of ancient bronze vessels decorated with patterns and symbols, and so I looked for words about the endurance of language.

a, noir corset velu des mouches éclatantes

The hermetic poetry of "Voyelles," a famous poem by Arthur Rimbaud, tempts the reader to skip rational explanations. Its critical analyses are very clever and interesting, but often depreciative. As a matter of fact, an intellectual understanding of the poem does not yield the key to this masterpiece. Only obsessively reading the poem aloud, listening to its words' music, brings out its poetic meaning.

My graphic interpretation does not try to explain the poem but rather to find a personal, sensitive correspondence: five vowels, five colors, five abstract human forms that express the sound of the letters through their attitudes. The transparency of the sheet of paper offers different levels of reading, and several versions of the woodcuts mirror Rimbaud's freedom in his poetry.

I created this artist's book with my regular collaborator, the graphic designer Enzo Messi, who made the book's cover and printed the woodcuts.

Claire Nydegger (Swiss, b. 1960)
Voyelles (Vowels), 1992

Poem by Arthur Rimbaud

Woodcuts and wood engravings on paper,

offset on paper and tracing paper

6.5 x 12.75 in.

Edition of 30; published by the artist, Saint-Prex, Switzerland

Gift of Gabriela Eigensatz and Yvana Enzler

Debra Weier (American, b. 1954)

A Merz Sonata, 1985

Poem by Jerome Rothenberg

Etching, rubber stamp, collage, screenprint, handmade paper

8.25 x 11.5 in.

Edition of 50; Emanon Press, Princeton Junction, New Jersey, and Women's Studio Workshop, Rosendale, New York

Gift of Ann D. Mitchell

I introduced poetry into my work early in my career. I found that my inspiration was fueled by collaborating with poets and building on another person's ideas. In my books I incorporate many media, depending on the content of the poems. *A Merz Sonata* was created in collaboration with the poet Jerome Rothenberg as a tribute to the German artist and poet Kurt Schwitters. A Dada master, Schwitters created collage assemblages he called *Merz*. Collage is the major visual element in this book, which includes glued bits of paper, ticket stubs, string, and rubber-stamped images. These tactile elements create an atmosphere of joy and surprise to counterbalance the feeling of anxiety and unrest prevalent in the poem.

Ámbar Past (Mexican, b. United States 1949)

Incantations by Mayan Women, 2005

Translated from Tzotzil into Spanish and English by Ámbar Past

Silkscreen and offset

10 x 10 in.

Edition of 200; Taller Leñateros, San Cristóbal de las Casas, Chiapas, Mexico

Gift of Lynn M. Johnston

I live among the Tzotzil Maya in the highlands of Chiapas, Mexico, where mud huts are filled with ritual poetry for making magic. Many of the verses refer to ancient books that were destroyed by the Spanish conquistadors yet remain in the collective unconscious of the Maya. The ancient Maya had a highly advanced written language and filled libraries with great collections of books. Women are thought to have been contributors to this culture of literacy; artifacts exist that depict Mayan women reading glyph books, and scholars believe some women functioned as scribes. The Spanish destroyed most Mayan volumes, leaving only three or four complete books that survive today. *Incantations by Mayan Women* may be the first book written, illustrated, printed, and bound—in paper of their own making—by the Maya in more than five hundred years, and it is the first volume of Mayan women's poetry ever published.

It took more than thirty years and 150 people to make *Incantations by Mayan Women*, an anthology of Mayan women's songs and spells that are illustrated by the authors' own spirit paintings. The cover depicts the Mayan goddess Kaxail and was designed and cast by Norwegian sculptor Gitte Daehlin. It was reproduced by the Mayan people of Taller Leñateros (Woodlanders Workshop) using recycled cardboard stained with coffee.

Karen Kunc (American, b. 1952)

Small Gifts, 2004

Text from Finnish folk song

Color etchings and aquatints on handmade paper, letterpress

3.5 x 5.5 in.

Edition of 18; Blue Heron Press, Avoca, Nebraska

Gift of Lynn M. Johnston

I created and proofed the etchings for *Small Gifts* while living with friends in Finland. The rich colors and details reflect the seasonal transition of light and the arrival of life. The special aura of the Scandinavian holiday Midsummer is captured—and literally etched—for a handheld memory. The text is from a Finnish folk song: "One month from the skylark, a fortnight from the finch, a few days from the wagtail, the swallow brings the summer in."

Linda Smith (American, b. 1948)
Inside Chance, 2000

Text by Alberto Ríos

Letterpress, digitally composed type, relief line engravings on paper; globe cast from

pigmented cotton linters, acrylic

4 x 4 x 4 in.

Edition of 100; Picnic Press, Phoenix, Arizona

Gift of NMWA Members' Art Acquisition Fund

Based on the magic cube, *Inside Chance* first takes on the appearance of a die. Eight small cubes are hinged to one another to make up one larger cube, inside of which a paper globe can be seen. To read the poem by Alberto Ríos, the reader opens the cube. Surfaces connect and break away in unexpected ways, rearranging the text into various configurations, with each manipulation conveying a different meaning. Altogether, there are twenty-six possible combinations. After the book moves through all of its possible shapes it returns to the die form. When the die is inverted, the original eight lines of the poem are revealed, one line per cube. Even though the text is linear it only works if it is written in a circle. The book is square and round at the same time; it opens in a line but circles around and around. This physical metaphor describes and demonstrates how, by chance, we all influence and change each other and the world in which we live.

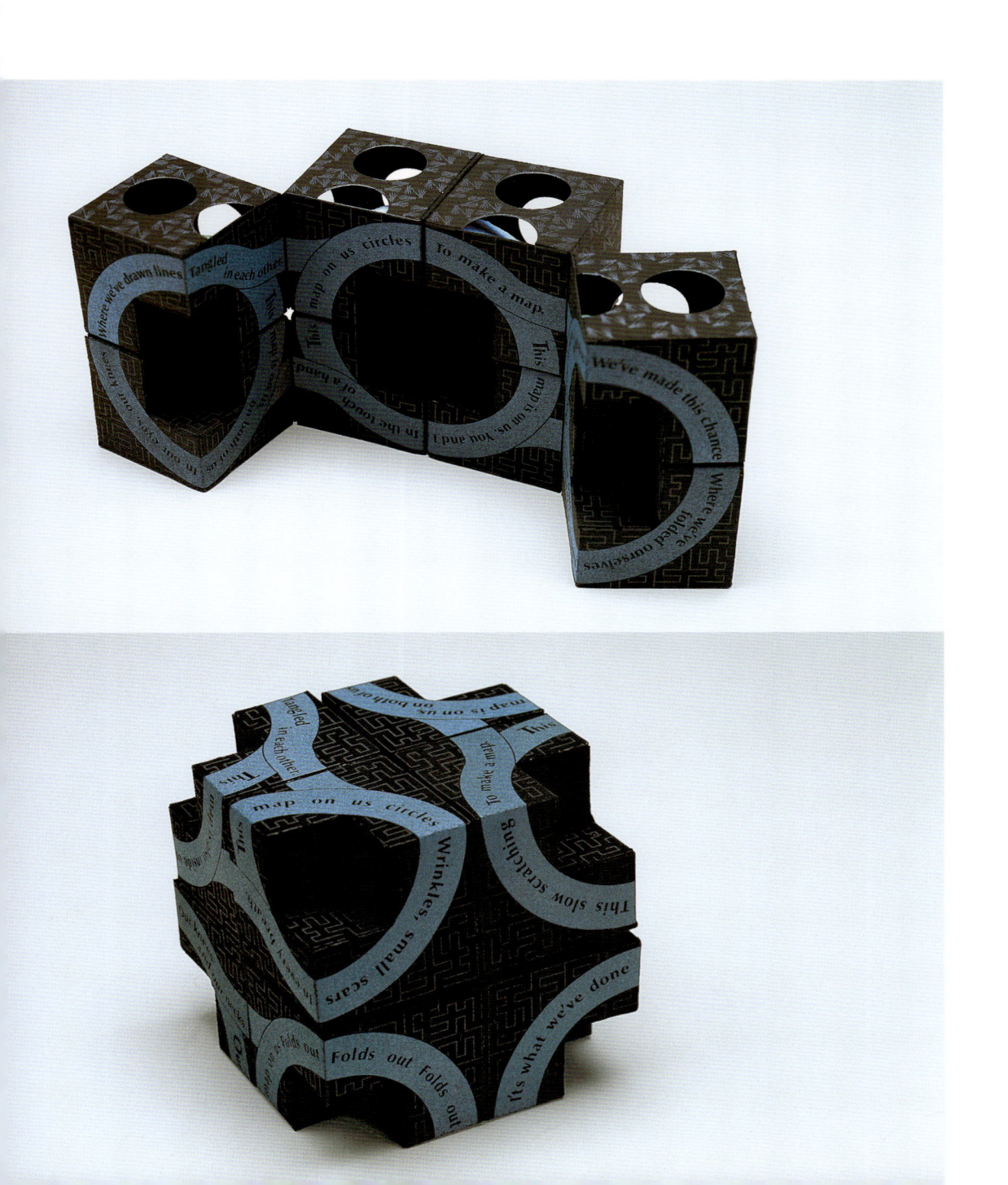

Elena Presser (American, b. Argentina 1940)

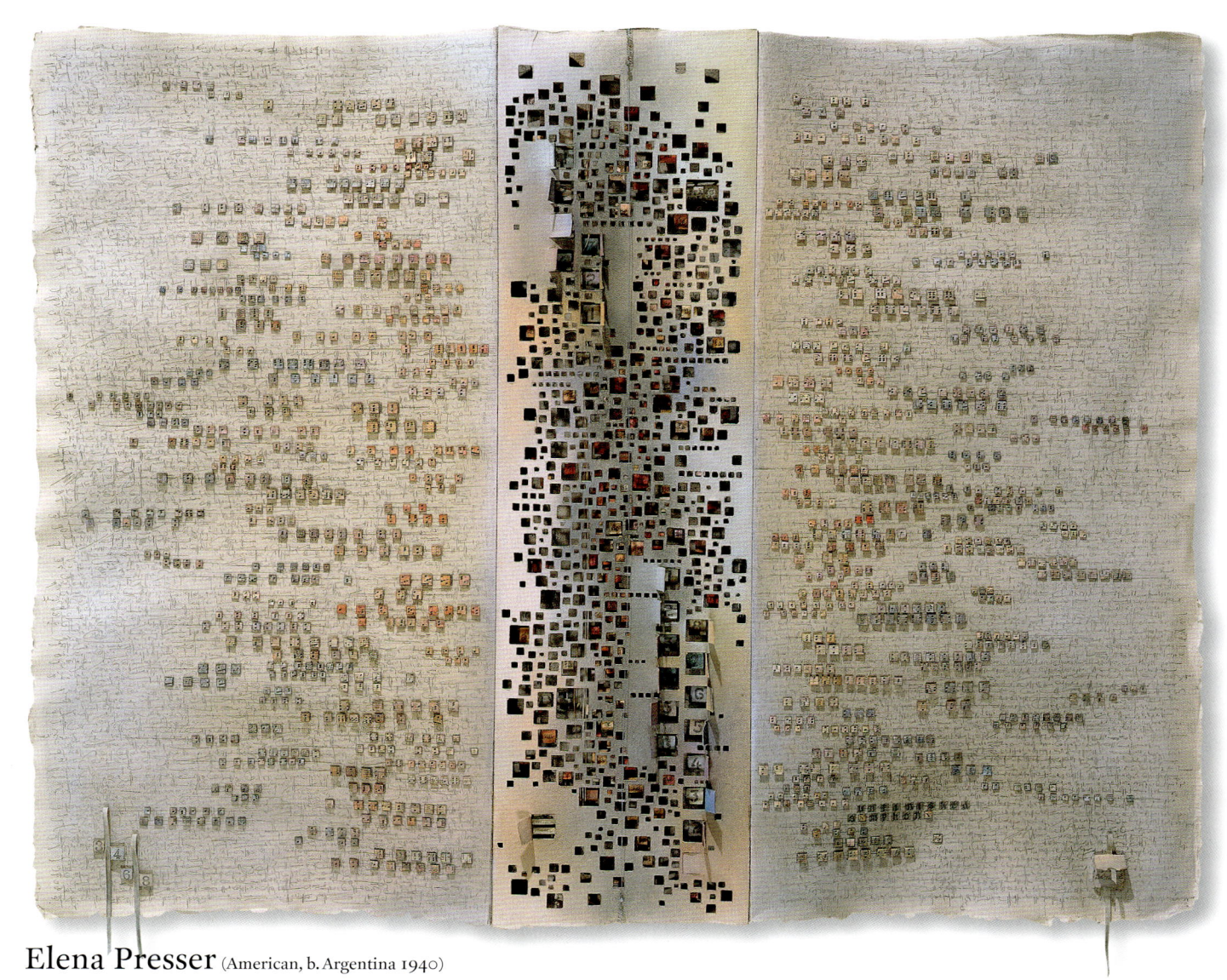

Unfinished Symphony, 1982

Paper, pastel, pencil, silk thread, silk ribbon, wire

36 x 29 in.

Unique artist's book

Gift of NMWA Members' Art Acquisition Fund and the artist

I perceive music as the most abstract form of art, and my concern is to convey musical abstraction as visual interpretation. *Unfinished Symphony* became a visual reality following a conversation I had with a friend, a lover of art and music. He transferred to me his excitement and enjoyment of this piece by Franz Schubert. "There is a crescendo that builds up into ecstasy," he said. "Schubert holds you there and then releases you."

The first movement of the symphony, which contains both quiet melancholy and agitated tragedy, is represented as the center of my work. Schubert suppressed the main theme at the start of the recapitulation in order to use it with greater force for the coda of the movement. I used the account of a dream that Schubert wrote down in the form of dramatic chords. Filled with melancholia and tragedy, the energy explodes through the squares and scroll of dreams. The second movement of the symphony, composed of two principal melodies, is music of the loveliest serenity. Two symmetrical sides of the book reach out from the central first movement and overflow with lyrical attributes. The small musical-score squares describe the mysterious quality and unfathomable beauty of the second movement.

François Villon has always fascinated me. He was a thief, a vagabond, and a great poet. I wanted to reinterpret his well-known "Ballad of the Hangmen" using the mystery of silhouettes and a shadow box. My friend Mick Stern, a poet who studied Villon, wrote a new translation of the poem, and I created the book in a display shadow box covered with earth, a reminder of a line from Villon's poem "Le grand testament," "De terre vint, en terre tourne" (who from earth comes, to earth returns). The display can be viewed in the box or as a stand that casts shadows. The papercut is enclosed within two windowed boxes, and the poem is handwritten with a rusty nib on a rough, handmade paper that recalls the hangmen's ropes.

Béatrice Coron (American, b. France 1956)
La ballade des pendus (Ballad of the hangmen), 1998

Poem by François Villon

Papercuts, shadow box, glass, electric bulb, wire, velvet paper, Indian handmade paper, ink, rust, book cloth, sand

9.75 x 15 in.

Edition of 5; published by the artist, New York City

Gift of Lorraine Grace

Karen Kunc (American, b. 1952)

Offering Time, 2001

Songs by Rabindranath Tagore

Book: color woodcuts on Japanese Nishinouchi paper, letterpress, intaglio printed dots, watercolor washes; box: sharkskin paper covered folio box

6.75 x 8 in.

Edition of 50; Blue Heron Press, Avoca, Nebraska

Gift of Lynn M. Johnston

The Bengali songs of Rabindranath Tagore, translated into English in 1913, provide the text for this artist's book. The songs pursue an understanding of time and acceptance of one's place in the eternal cycle. I found inspiration for this book in visual impressions from travel to Bangladesh as well as key images from Tagore's words: the evolution of a wildflower, a maze of shadows and light, a red lotus, and a winding path. The book as a whole creates a falling pathway of color and image that evokes the patterns of the passage of time.

L'Invitation au voyage is a folded painting that seeks to illuminate rather than illustrate the well-known poem by Charles Baudelaire. The gouache highlighted with pastel was done on a long piece of colored Japanese hemp paper, which was then lined and folded accordion-style into a book form and attached to paper-covered boards. It can be read page by page or viewed as a long picture, like a scroll. The simple block printing of the text is inscribed over and within the painting, from which it becomes inseparable. I chose to use this unadorned lettering in contrast to the more ornate painted background in order that the poem be seen clearly as the author's poem and not a work of calligraphy.

The decision to make a book around this particular poem seemed almost inevitable because of the haunting beauty of its imagery and the soulful music of its words. Although I made this book in 1998, the poem has been present in the back of my mind since I first learned to read it in French during a year of study in Paris in 1953–54. It is always a challenge to do something with a work that is so widely appreciated; to me, the poem's universal quality is attractive, opening the text to many individual interpretations.

Anne Walker (French, b. United States 1933)

L'Invitation au voyage, (Invitation to a voyage), 1998

Poem by Charles Baudelaire

Gouache and pastel on paper

3.75 x 7 in.

Unique artist's book

Gift of Lois Pollard Price

Having always been irritated by egotism and excessive self-absorption, I found myself at the height of displeasure in Paris upon seeing I. M. Pei's seventy-one-foot-high glass pyramid sitting in the middle of the Louvre's Cour Napoleon. Totally captivated by ancient sites, I responded to the then-broiling controversy by determining this structure to be a grossly misplaced monolith. Given Pei's training in the United States, his architectural statement seemed to reflect the American propensity to fill every available space on an ego-driven excursion. Pei's poorly positioned pyramid provided the perfect point of departure from which I could expound.

I employed both European and American icons, executed in drawing and collage, and in Duchampian fashion I penned puns in French and English. Occasionally wordplay suggests a fierceness, as seen in one illustration of a large pyramid sitting on a *peluche* (plush) chair about to *imperil* (impale) the next person who would attempt to take a seat. Images of pyramids permeate *Peiload*, just as extreme concern for oneself impregnates our society. The importance of the effect of overabundance is addressed by a proliferation of pointed shards commanding total attention in a disruptive manner, much like Pei's pyramid dominates the once refreshing open space in the center of the Louvre.

Jo-Anne Echevarria-Myers (American, b. 1944)

Peiload, 1989

Offset, letterpress

8.25 x 8.25 in.

Edition of 100; published by the artist, Cape May, New Jersey

Gift of the artist

M. L. Van Nice (American, b. 1945)

Swiss Army Book, 1990

Ink on paper, linen, wood, pen nib, ribbon

20.25 x 11.5 x 8.75 in. (open)

Unique artist's book

Gift of Lois Pollard Price

We're all familiar with the Swiss Army knife that opens blade after blade, clown-car fashion, to reveal an inventory that runs the gizmo-gamut from feather plucker to garden rake. It is, at the last, a small hinged tool chest running far amok of anything Webster might have called "knife." *Swiss Army Book* is the tool book of knowledge. It is a volume both of knowledge and of tools necessary for the modification of that knowledge.

Conclusions of science are final; we know them as facts. But in a world without boundaries, all things are possible and nothing is final. Knowledge seems to have a shelf-life. In his day, Pliny the Elder knew just about everything there was to know, including the fact that pearls are the offspring of shells made pregnant by dew; two thousand years of addition and subtraction to the sum of his knowledge have made poetry of Pliny's work.

Swiss Army Book is a simple trope: Here is the written word; burn the written word; rewrite the written word; leave matches for the next guy.

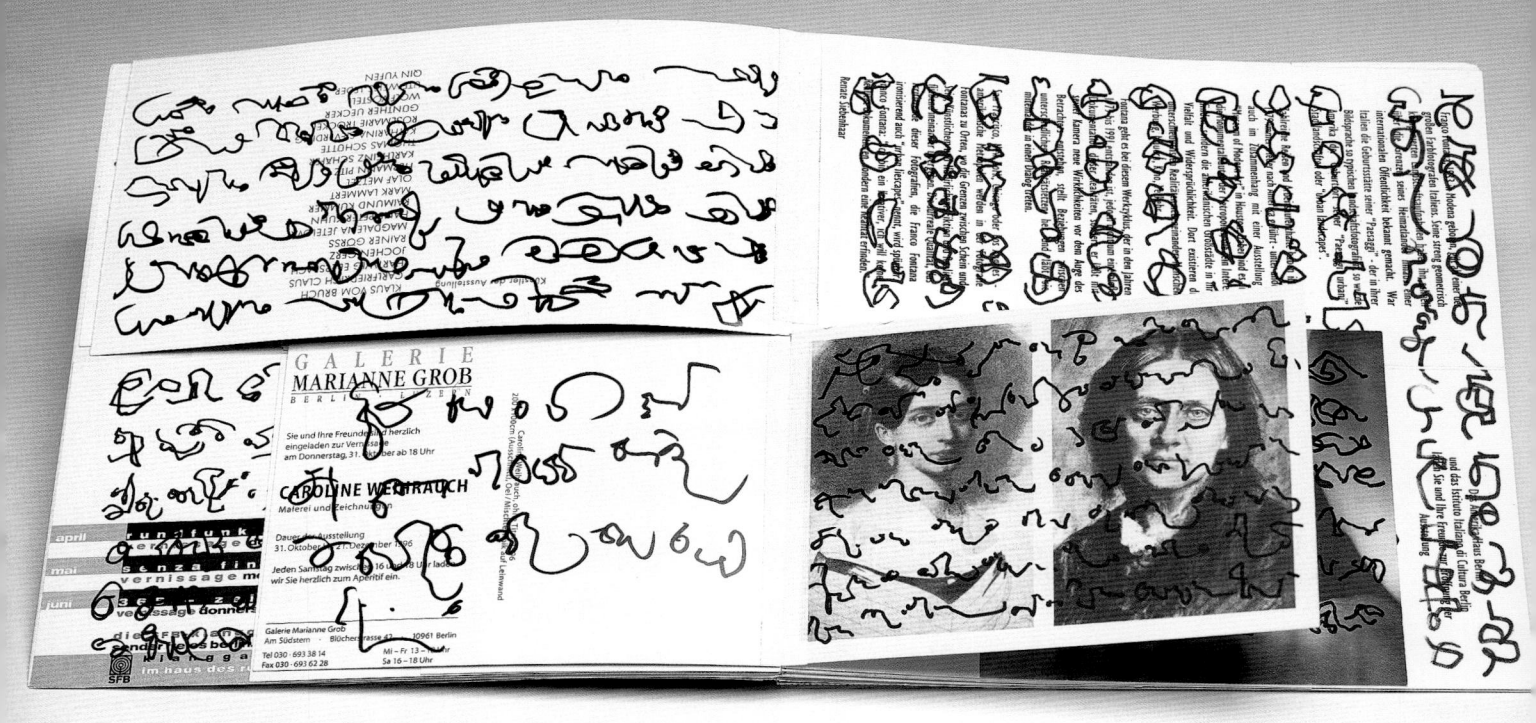

Karla Woisnitza (German, b. 1952)

Einladung (Invitation), 1998

Invitations, ink and graphite drawings, linen

8.5 x 8.5 in.

Unique artist's book

Gift of the artist

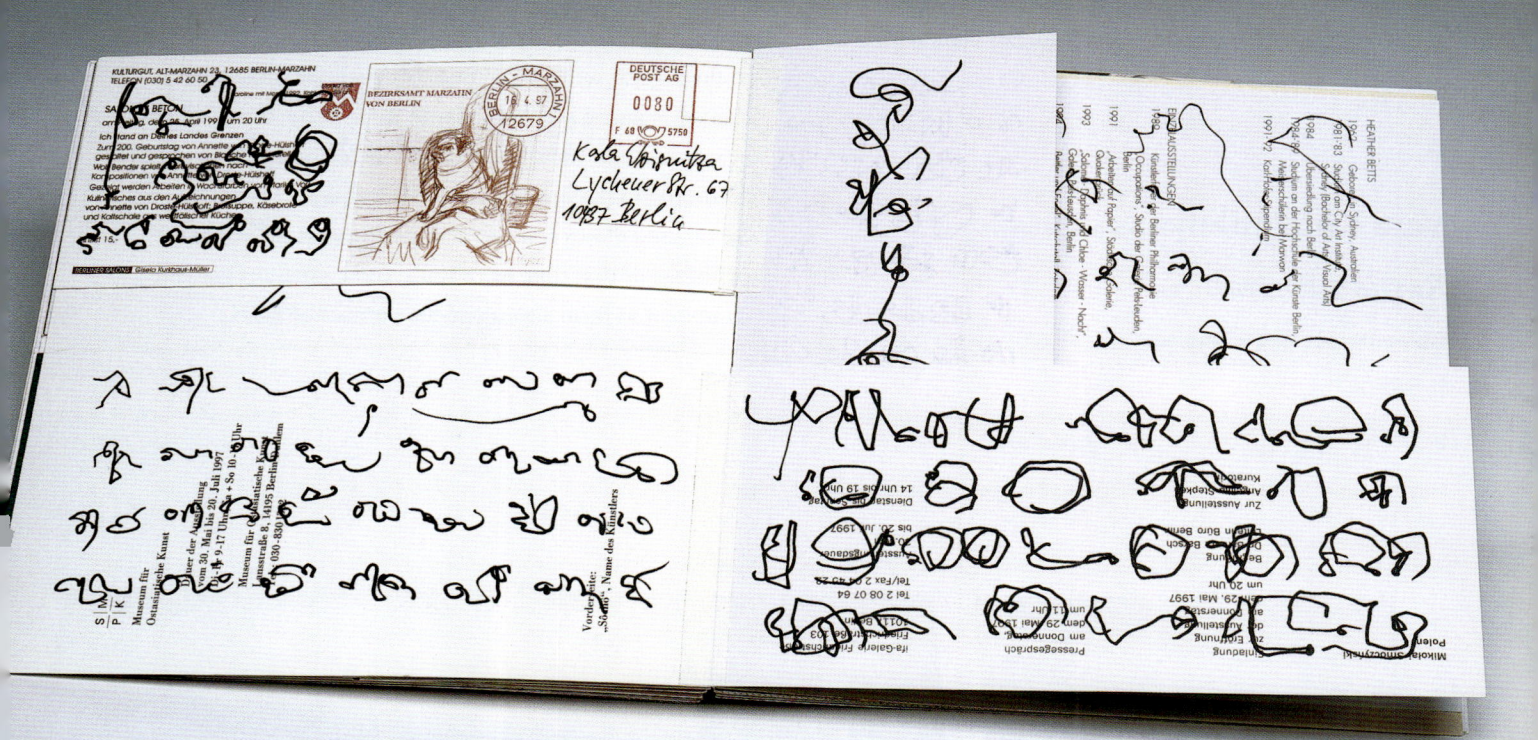

Einladung consists entirely of invitation postcards for exhibitions that I received over a period of time while living in Berlin. Beautiful and distinctly designed by other artists, these wonderful and intricate compositions serve to announce music, speeches, and discussions, promoting ideas of colorful activity, communication, and living space.

During this time in Berlin, I did my daily drawings not as usual on white paper but directly on the cards with a pencil, thus engaging in the texts themselves while simultaneously infusing them with my own artistry. My personal signs on the cards result in a sort of meandering path through those artists' exhibitions.

185

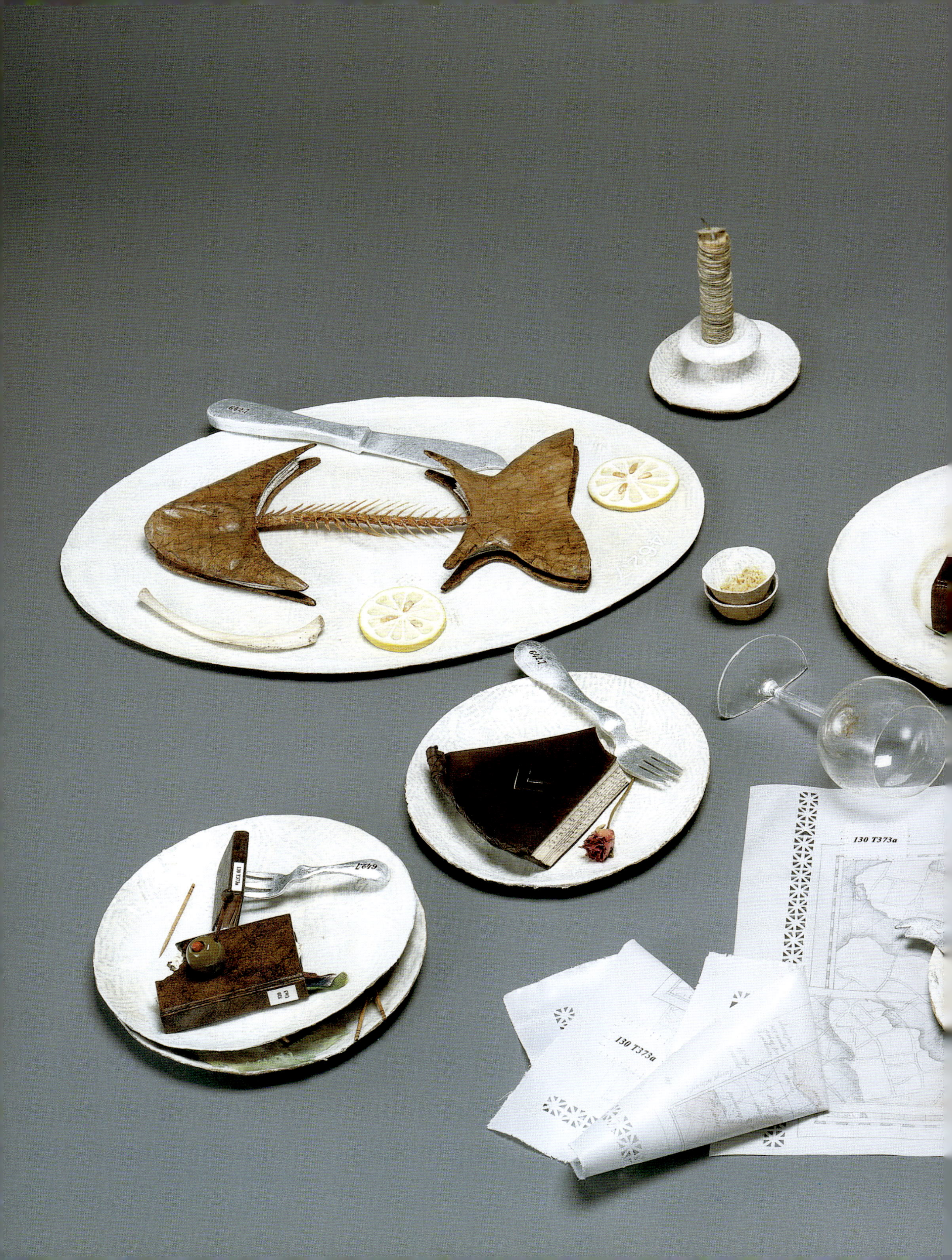
6427
130 T373a
130 T373a

O
Octopus, 28
Offering Time, 172
Ojeda, Naúl, 176-77
Oleszko, Pat, 38-39
On a Darkling Plain, 110-11
On the Line, 48-49
On This Land, 136-37
Oppenheim, Meret, 154-55
Ordinary/Extraordinary, 117
Ovubet (26 Girls with Sweet Centers), 32-33
Owen, Jan, 156-57

P
Past, Ámbar, 162-63, 176-77
Pecanins, Yani, 107
Peiload, 180
Penn, Beverly, 56-57
Perrin, Mary, 120
Presser, Elena, 168
Privacy, 36-37

R
Reading Dick and Jane with Me, 106
The Reptilian Brain, 114-15
Residue, 40
RIM, 52
Rosenberg, Maddy, 94-95
Russian Portrait, 186

S
Schwartzott, Carol, 139
Seven Windows, 46-47
Shadow of Descent, 94-95
Shadow Play, 170-71
Share, Susan Joy, 64
Sharoff, Shirley, 148-49
She Has Vanished from the Outside and Gone Within..., 76-77
"She keeps her secrets in an amber jar so the light won't fade them," 85
Shenitzer, Miriam, 182
Shenk, Genie, 2-3, 90-91
Silk and Secrecy, 41
Sleeping Inside the Glacier, 142-43
Sligh, Clarissa, 106, 121
Small Gifts, 164-65
Smith, Linda, 166-67

The Snake, 59
Soap Story, 45
Sollod, Ellen, 144
Song Lines, 134-35
Spitzmueller, Pamela, 80-81
Stevens, May, 117
Stones of Sorrow, 61
Storer, Inez, 42-43
Stout, Renée, 46-47
Sweren, Betty, 59
Swiss Army Book, 181

T
Teatimes, 63
Thiewes, Rachelle, 56-57
Tierney, M. Jordan, 85
Todaro, Carol, 79, 123
Treading the Maze, an Artist's Book of Daze, 78
True to Life, 29
Tunnel Map, 130

U
The Uneventful Life of Doña Carmen y Constanza, 42-43
Unfinished Symphony, 168

V
Van Nice, M.L., 181, 187-89
Van Vliet, Claire, 89, 178-79
Volo-volume (Flight-volume), 124
Voyelles (Vowels), 158-59

W
Walker, Anne, 173
Walker, Kara, 44
Waltzing Matilda, 138
Wascher-James, Sande, 99
Watanabe, Kazuko, 126-27
Watson, Brenda, 54-55
Webb, Philippa, 138
Weier, Debra, 160-61
Weinstein, Joyce Ellen, 34-35
What's Happening with Momma?, 121
Wheeling, 103
Woisnitza, Karla, 184-85
Woman concerned in art..., 30-31
Women and Cars, 74-75
Wonder Production, Volume I, 96-97
The World after September 11, 2001: A Reinforced Book, 112